The Via Algarviana

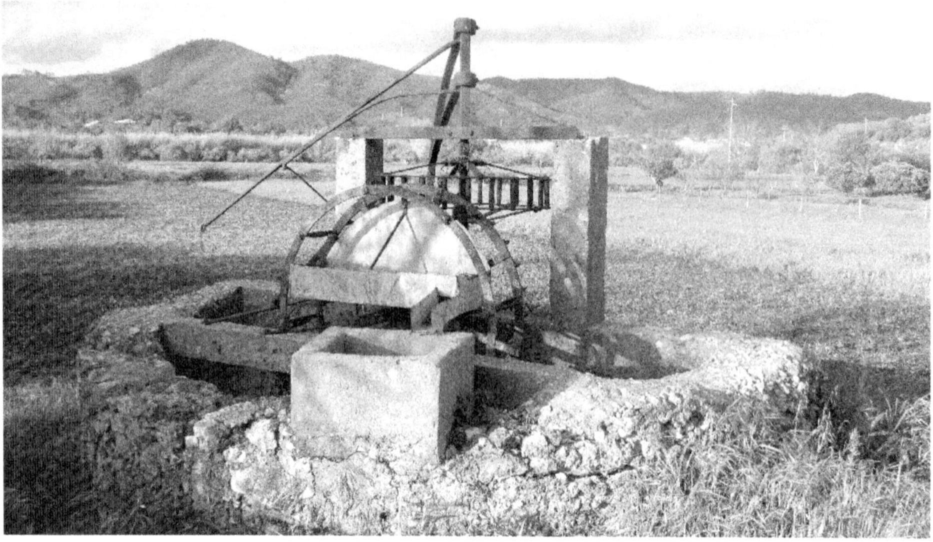

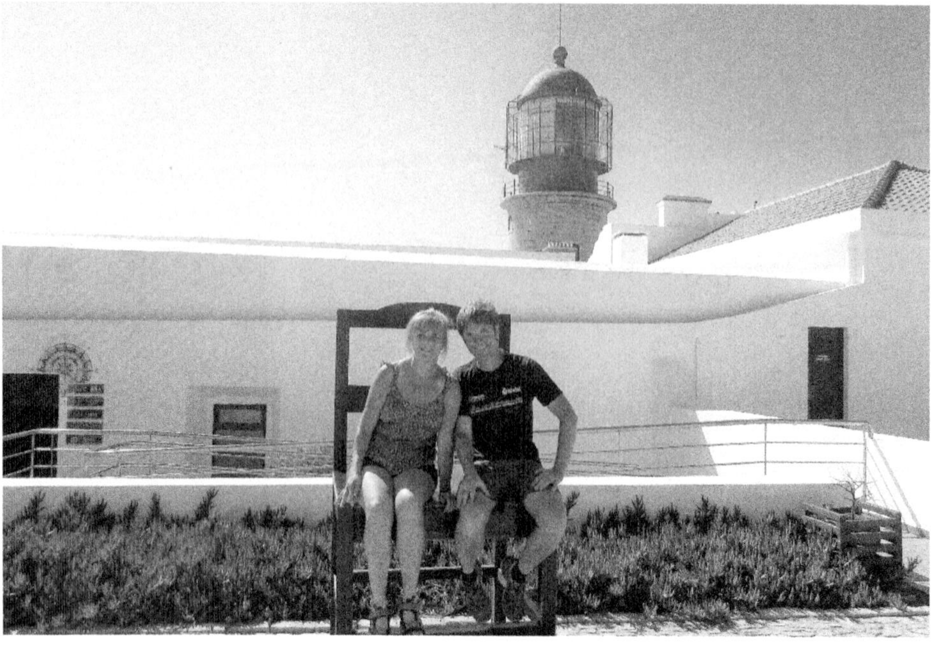

The Via Algarviana

An English guide to the 'Algarve Way'

by Harri Garrod Roberts

Copyright 2015 Harri Garrod Roberts

All right reserved

ISBN-13: 9781796958904

Contents

Introduction	7
Practicalities	15
How to use this guide	25
The Via Algarviana (GR13)	27
Distances	31
Day 1: Alcoutim to Balurcos	32
Day 2: Balurcos to Furnazinhas	38
Day 3: Furnazinhas to Vaqueiros	43
Day 4: Vaqueiros to Cachopo	48
Day 5: Cachopo to Barranco do Velho	53
Day 6: Barranco do Velho to Salir	61
Day 7: Salir to Alte	67
Day 8: Alte to São Bartolomeu de Messines	73
Day 9: São Bartolomeu de Messines to Silves	79
Day 10: Silves to Monchique	84
Day 11: Monchique to Marmelete	91
Day 12: Marmelete to Barão de São Jão	96
Day 13: Barão de São Jão to Vila do Bispo	102
Day 14: Vila do Bispo to Cabo de São Vicente	107
Alternative finish	111
Day 12: Marmelete to Aljezur	112
Day 13: Aljeur to Affifana	116
Day 14: Arrifana to Carrapateira	120
Day 15: Carrapateira to Vila do Bispo	125
Day 16: Vila do Bispo to Cabo de São Vicente	130
The Via Algarviana: walking 300km across the Algarve	135
Never too old to backpack: More Algarve hiking	136

O Fôn i Fynwy: Walking Wales from end to end	137
Never Too Old To Backpack: a 364-mile walk through Wales	138
Other books by Harri Garrod Roberts	139
About the author	140

Introduction

The bustling resorts and sandy beaches of Portugal's Algarve region are well known to visitors, who flock in their thousands each year to enjoy one of the most reliably sunny climates in Europe. A short distance inland, however, is a very different Algarve, and one that has only recently been discovered by walkers from northern Europe. Here you will find a varied landscape of rolling hills, dry orchards, cork forests, and agricultural terraces. Sleepy, unspoilt towns and villages offer a fascinating glimpse into the Algarve's cultural heritage while also providing an opportunity to sample the region's hospitality and rich culinary traditions.

Threading its way through the hills from settlement to settlement is the Via Algarviana ('Algarve Way'), a waymarked, long-distance trail stretching the entire length of the Algarve, from the Spanish border in the east to the Atlantic Ocean in the west. The 300km (186-mile) journey along this trail is an unforgettable experience and provides an introduction to an Algarve that few visitors ever get to see. This book describes the complete route from Alcoutim to Cabo de São Vicente (Cape St Vincent), as well as an alternative finish to the walk via Aljezur and the Rota Vicentina – another long-distance trail exploring southern Portugal's windswept Atlantic coast.

Location

The Algarve is located in the far south of Portugal and is the only Portuguese region with both south- and west-facing coasts. At the juncture of the two coastlines is Cabo de São Vicente or Cape St Vincent, the most south-westerly point of mainland Europe; in medieval times it was known as 'the end of the world'. To the north, the region borders the Portuguese province of Alentejo, while to the east, across the Guadiana river, is the Spanish region of Andalucía.

In shape, the Algarve resembles an elongated rectangle. Its longest sides run from west to east across the full width of Portugal – a distance of some 130km (80 miles) as the crow flies. The shortest distance widthways across the region – from north to south – is as little as 30km (18 miles) in places, but is generally closer to 40km (25 miles). In total, the region covers an area of just under 5,000km^2 (1,929 square miles) – between around 5 and 6 per cent of mainland Portugal.

Brief history of the Algarve

Early humans are believed to have roamed the Iberian peninsula over a million years ago, and the region later became a stronghold for Europe's Neanderthal population. Around 40,000BC modern humans began to move into the peninsula from southern France, displacing the indigenous Neanderthals. Hunter-gatherer cultures continued to dominate the peninsula until around 4000BC, when the adoption of agriculture led to the development of more complex societies. The megaliths left by these people were the first permanent man-made structures to be built in the Algarve and are particularly prevalent in the coastal area around Vila do Bispo.

In the first millennium BC, Iberia was invaded by several waves of Celts from Central Europe, who mingled with indigenous populations to form numerous new tribes. Southern Portugal was dominated by the Conii, an Iron Age people who are known to have traded with the Mediterranean civilizations of the Phoenicians and the Carthaginians. Phoenician adventurers had established trading posts along the region's south coast as early as

1000BC, while the Carthaginians founded what is today Portimão around 550BC.

In 219BC, Roman troops entered Iberia for the first time, initiating a brutal guerrilla war that was to last 200 years. By 19BC, the Roman Republic controlled almost the entire peninsula and had incorporated most of what was later to become Portugal into the province of Lusitania. Their old enemies from the Punic Wars, the Carthaginians, were expelled from the province and their coastal colonies taken over. A focal point for Roman settlement was Lagos, with its important harbour, and several Roman ruins have been found in the area.

Roman rule came to an abrupt end with the Visigoth invasion of the fifth century. Although originally a Germanic tribe, the Visigoths had long since adopted Roman language and culture, and their kingdom helped to consolidate the Latinization of Iberia. In 711, however, a small force of Arabs and Berbers landed near Gibraltar, beginning an invasion that would bring almost the entire peninsula under Muslim control by the end of the century. These Islamic invaders called their new territory Al-Andalus; the Algarve was Gharb Al-Andalus or simply Al-Gharb, meaning 'the west'. Its most prominent city was Silves, which became so wealthy under Moorish rule that it became known as 'the Baghdad of the West'. The splendid castle built by the city's Moorish rulers continues to dominate Silves to this day.

In the mid 12th century, the newly established Kingdom of Portugal began a series of successful military campaigns in the Algarve, pushing south into the region as part of the Christian Reconquista. By the middle of the following century, the Algarve had been secured by the Portuguese, and King Afonso III had begun to style himself King of Portugal and the Algarve. Although the Algarve became fully integrated into the Portuguese kingdom, it retained its status as a distinct possession of the Portuguese

Crown right up to the proclamation of the Portuguese Republic in 1910.

In the 15th century, Prince Henry the Navigator established a naval base at Sagres, in the west of the Algarve, and launched a series of maritime expeditions that helped to establish Portugal as a major colonial power. The proceeds of trade, loot and slavery brought great wealth to the Algarve, particularly into its capital Lagos, which was also the region's principal port. The famous Lisbon earthquake of 1755 caused tremendous destruction along the Algarve coast, which was devastated by an enormous tsunami that produced waves higher than Lagos's city walls. Protected by the sandy banks of the Ria Formosa, the city of Faro remained relatively unscathed, allowing it to acquire the title of regional capital in the years that followed.

In 1910, a revolution led to the overthrow of the Portuguese monarchy and the founding of a republic. Political instability resulted in the establishment of a military dictatorship in 1926, which survived until the 'Carnation Revolution' of 1974 restored democracy in a largely bloodless coup. The launch of the coup on 25 April is still celebrated each year as a national holiday.

Since the 1970s, tourism has become a major industry in Portugal, particularly in the Algarve – a region that has also attracted a large number of expats from Britain and elsewhere in northern Europe. Economic development, however, has been largely concentrated along the coast, exacerbating the problems of stagnation and depopulation in many inland communities. The Almargem association, founded in 1988, works to promote sustainable development in all areas of the Algarve, as well as protect the region's unique cultural and environmental heritage. Through the provision of well-marked walking trails in the Algarve (including the Via Algarviana), Almargem hopes to promote walking as an activity in the region and provide much-needed tourism opportunities for local businesses.

Landscape

The landscape of the Algarve can be divided into three distinct types: *serra, barrocal* and coast. Although the Via Algarviana passes through numerous examples of the first two types, the only coastal landscapes explored by the trail are on the final day's walking. An alternative finish, via Aljezur and along the Rota Vicentina (GR11), provides an opportunity to explore the west coast of the Algarve more thoroughly.

The *serra* is the name for the area of hills and mountains stretching across the northern half of the Algarve, along the border with the Alentejo region. These occupy approximately half the total area of the Algarve and consist of three different ranges. The most extensive is the Serra do Caldeirão, in the centre and east of the Algarve: an area of wild, undulating hills clothed in scrub and cork woodland and reaching a high point of a little under 600m. Abutting these to the west is the Serra de Monchique, dominated by the Algarve's two highest peaks, Fóia (902m) and Picota (774m). This is a very special place of forest and heathland with a truly alpine feel. Further west again, the high mountains dwindle into the Serra de Espinhaço de Cão, an area of gentle coastal hills bordering the Costa Vicentina (see below).

The *barrocal* is the name given to the Algarve's fertile agricultural region between the narrow coastal strip and the hilly uplands of the serra. Here historic paths meander between groves of olives and citrus and past orchards of figs and almonds. Ancient walls border fertile vegetable plots, still irrigated from wells first sunk by the Moors. Prosperous market towns such as São Bartolomeu de Messines act as distribution centres for the region's agricultural produce. A good place to look out over the surrounding barrocal landscape is from the castle walls at Silves.

The Algarve's narrow coastal strip (known as the littoral) is where most of the region's tourist activities are concentrated. Nevertheless, between the resorts can be found many rich and diverse landscapes, including dunes, pine forests and saltwater lagoons. In the far west, the coastline becomes more rugged, with spectacular limestone cliffs a notable feature to the west of Lagos. The Algarve's western coast, north of Cabo de São Vicente, is known as the Costa Vicentina and consists of rugged, windswept cliffs punctuated by numerous small sandy bays. This is a region largely unspoilt by tourism and is explored more fully by another long-distance trail in the Algarve, the Rota Vicentina. Walkers on the Via Algarviana can connect with the Rota Vicentina at Aljezur quite easily, providing an alternative coastal route for the final few days' walking on the trail.

Wildlife and habitats

Although bordering the Atlantic, the Algarve possesses many of the climatic and ecological characteristics of a Mediterranean climate, with mild, wet winters and hot, dry summers ideally suited to plant life. Indeed, it has been estimated that Mediterranean climates provide a home to a staggering 20 per cent of all plant species in the world – a level of diversity surpassed only in the tropical rainforests. The best time to appreciate this diversity is in the spring, particularly between the months of February and April, when wild flower meadows throughout the Algarve are ablaze with colour. These vibrant displays of flowering plants attract equally colourful butterflies and moths, as well as less noticeable insects, which in turn provide a source of food for a tremendous variety of birds, reptiles, amphibians and mammals.

Among the many flowering plants visible in springtime are at least 30 species of orchid. These include several varieties of bee orchid, which mimic various species of female insects so as to trick amorous male insects into attempting to mate with them (a pollination strategy known as pseudocopulation). There are also other attractive species such as the broad-leaved helleborine and the intriguingly named naked man orchid (so called because its petals supposedly look like naked men). For a better understanding of the full range of wild flowers to be found in the Algarve, try the following two books: **Wildflowers in the Algarve**, by Pat O'Reilly and Sue Parker, and *Wild Orchids of the Algarve,* by Sue Parker.

Much of the Algarve's native tree cover has been replaced by fast-growing eucalyptus trees, which provide a ready supply of wood pulp for the paper industry. They do not support a great deal of wildlife, however, and their slowly rotting leaves form a dense carpet which tends to stifle many native species of plants and fungi. Better for wildlife are the areas of mixed oak and pine that can be found dotted around various parts of the Algarve. Along the Via Algarviana, the best examples of this type of mixed woodland are to be found on the hills above Monchique. The other major type of woodland to be found in the Algarve is stone pine, a tough species which grows well in arid coastal conditions. There is a large protected stone pine forest to the north-west of Barão de São João.

Visitors from Britain will recognize many familiar bird species, such as the house martin and swallow, though these tend to congregate in far greater numbers than is normal in northern Europe. A more exotic sight is that of white storks nesting on urban chimneys and the brightly coloured plumage of the European bee-eater. In mountain areas you may be lucky enough to spot vultures or short-toed eagles, while the coast around Cabo de São Vicente is a great place to spot all manner of migratory birds. Good information on what can be seen when can be found in *Algarve Wildlife*, by Clive Viney and Ray Tipper.

The Algarve's Mediterranean climate supports a wider range of reptiles and amphibians than is found in northern Europe. These include several species of salamander, newts, frogs and toads, as well as snakes, lizards and terrapins. Particularly common are the Iberian water frog, whose loud croaks can be heard wherever freshwater occurs, and the Moorish gecko, a robust-looking lizard often found in houses. In summer, the large Montpellier snake may be seen slithering across roads (where it is frequently killed), while streams and river pools provide a home for the viperine snake and Spanish terrapin. In total, eight species of snake can be found in the Algarve, but none are considered particularly dangerous to humans.

Most mammals in the Algarve are nocturnal and secretive and unlikely to be encountered by walkers. Many mammal species found in the Algarve are common elsewhere in Europe, including in Britain, but there are also species introduced from north Africa, such as the Egyptian mongoose, a cat-sized mammal often active by day. Wild boar are common in the Algarve hills but are active mainly at night and unlikely to be seen. Two creatures that you will almost certainly not encounter are the Iberian wolf – hunted to extinction in the Algarve by 1920 – and the Iberian lynx. The world's rarest feline species, the Iberian lynx is known to number no more than a few hundred wild individuals, mainly in the neighbouring Spanish province of Andalucía. The animal's last Algarve stronghold is believed to have been in the wooded hills around Monchique, but it has been many years since the last confirmed sighting.

Practicalities

When to walk

The walking season in the Algarve is generally considered to run from September until June. Extremely high temperatures in July and August make walking difficult during daylight hours, and the landscape at this time of year is also at its most parched and barren. From September, temperatures start to gradually decline, though it can remain uncomfortably hot for walking even in October.

Cooler weather in November makes walking much easier, though as the month progresses the likelihood of rain also increases considerably. Rain in the Algarve is usually light, though torrential rain can also occur during severe winter storms. Between showers, however, you can expect many warm pleasant days, but be prepared for a sharp drop in temperature during the long winter nights.

Already by December, winter rains have begun to awaken dormant plants and spur growth in the soil. As the days lengthen, spring arrives with a blaze of colour, wild flower meadows springing up throughout the Algarve during February. The landscape is at its most beautiful between February and April, making this the best time of year to walk the Via Algarviana. The weather during this period should be pleasantly warm, without ever being uncomfortably hot. You will also have the advantage of lengthening days.

By May, the landscape begins to take on a more parched appearance, and climbing temperatures can make walking much harder. If walking in May or June, you are advised to set off early each day and to carry plenty of liquids.

Equipment

There are several companies that provide luggage transfers and logistical support along the Via Algarviana (for information visit www.algarvewalkingexperience.com or www.ramblersholidays.co.uk), but the cheapest and simplest way of walking the trail is as a continuous backpack, carrying everything you need. When walking unsupported in this way, the trick is to carry as little as possible while still managing not to leave anything essential behind.

To give you some idea of what you might need, I carried the following items during a continuous hike of the trail in May 2015 (some items were shared with my partner):

- Lightweight two-man tent (outer only)
- Groundsheet
- Sleeping bag, inflatable mat and pillow
- Camera, iPad, mobile, chargers and adaptors
- Sun hat and sunglasses
- Sun cream, lip balm and insect repellent
- Two one-litre water bottles
- Water filter
- Travel towel
- Two spare pairs of shorts
- Two spare pairs of socks
- Two spare lightweight T-shirts
- A spare long-sleeved top
- Flip-flops (I walked in Salomon trail running shoes)
- Toiletries
- Clothes pegs and elasticated line
- SwissCard pocket tool
- First aid kit
- Compass
- Head torch and lightweight handheld torch

- Spare batteries
- Baby wipes
- Pencil and paper
- Book to read
- Any additional food and drink we bought daily.

We took the tent primarily as a backup, in case we were unable to find alternative accommodation, but in the end it was not required (so neither were the groundsheet, sleeping mat, or pillow). The sleeping bag only got used once – in a hostel in Marmelete – but I could easily have made do with a sheet or sleeping bag liner, the weather was so hot. The result was that a large proportion of what I carried (in terms of weight) never actually got used. Nevertheless, taking the tent still seems the sensible thing to have done, given that we couldn't guarantee the availability of accommodation each night. It also allowed us to be flexible with regard to the distances we walked each day.

Two items I took the risk of not taking were a waterproof jacket and long trousers. This was a risk that paid off, as we enjoyed consistently high temperatures throughout our two-week trip, with only a small amount of light, patchy rain at the beginning of the walk. (One other reason often mentioned for wearing long trousers is to prevent bites from ticks, but this shouldn't be a problem on the Via Algarviana, which follows mainly wide tracks and very few narrow, overgrown paths.) All the places we stayed were very relaxed, and I never once felt 'underdressed' because I was wearing shorts and flip-flops when eating out in the evening. Of course, my choice of gear reflected what I knew about the Algarve climate in May; if walking in winter, I would certainly have chosen to take a waterproof, trousers and a fleece.

The consistently hot, sunny days were both a help and a hindrance when backpacking. On the plus side, the hot sunshine meant that dirty clothes could be swilled out and dried within the space of an hour or two (I could easily have got away with only one spare T-shirt and one spare pair of shorts, rather than two of each). There was also no need to pack away books, sleeping bags, and electronic items in waterproof bags. However, the physical demands of walking in a hot climate with very little shade should not be underestimated. Sun cream and lip balm were essential items of equipment, and a sun hat was also useful during the hottest part of the day. Even so, I found I had to wear a long-sleeved top early on in the walk to protect sunburnt arms. I also discovered that there's a limit to how much direct sunlight an iPad will put up with!

The most important to thing to remember when walking in hot weather is to carry plenty of water or other fluids. We ran out of water on one particularly long, hot day, despite carrying two one-litre water bottles each, plus extra bottled water. Although we didn't end up using the water filter, the experience demonstrated that we were right to take it. After that, we supplemented our water supplies for each day with cans of Sumo, a popular fizzy drink that was much more palatable than water when hot.

With regards to food, we rarely carried that much, as almost every day's walk ended at a place with a cafe, restaurant or grocery store (details of facilities available can be found in the route information box for each day). For emergencies, we carried a small supply of dry, non-perishable food (mainly nuts and Nature Valley granola bars).

Getting to the Algarve

The Algarve is one of the most popular holiday destinations in Europe, and if booked well in advance, there are cheap flights available to the region's capital, Faro, from airports throughout the UK. If flights to Faro are not available, it is also possible to fly into Lisbon and catch a train or coach to the Algarve. Tickets for these intercity services should be booked online in advance, as in summer or on weekends trains and coaches are often full. If travelling to the Algarve from Lisbon, it is worth checking out the following transport information website – www.algarvebus.info – run by a British expat. The site contains a comprehensive array of timetables and links, as well as useful information on how to get from the airport to a bus terminal.

Dangers

On the whole, Portugal is an extremely safe country to walk in. Nevertheless, it is always advisable to take certain basic precautions when hiking. Listed below are some of the possible dangers you may encounter, their likelihood, and what you can do to avoid them. In the event of an emergency, call 112 for assistance. It is also a good idea to obtain and carry a European Health Insurance Card and to take out adequate insurance cover.

Heat – This is without doubt the biggest threat to any walker's safety. Cover up, wear a sun hat, and apply sun cream to any exposed skin. Above all, carry plenty of water or other fluids – even three to four litres is not excessive on a very hot day. In hot weather, you may wish to consider starting early so as to avoid the worst of the afternoon heat (though this is not always convenient when staying in bed and breakfast accommodation).

Crime – Crime rates in rural Portugal are extremely low, and it is unlikely that you will find yourself a victim of crime while walking in the Algarve. Nevertheless, pickpocketing does occur, particularly around the larger coastal resorts, and when out and about you should always ensure that any money or valuables are kept safe and concealed.

Traffic – Several sections of the Via Algarviana are routed along public roads. Although these are generally very quiet by British standards, it is important to remember that drivers using them may not be expecting to encounter walkers. On roads with no pavement, it is generally advisable to walk on the left-hand side of the road, so as to face any oncoming traffic. The exception to this rule is on blind bends, where it is almost always safer to walk on the outside of the bend.

Bees – Beekeeping is a thriving rural industry in the Algarve, and you will pass numerous hives when walking the Via Algarviana. Keep your distance from any hives passed and carry antihistamines if you think you may be allergic to bee stings.

Wild boar – Wild boar are common in the Algarve hills and have a reputation for ferocity. However, they are active mainly at night, and you are unlikely to encounter any when walking.

Dogs – Nearly every rural property in the Algarve seems to have at least one dog. These may look and sound fierce, but the dog is almost always safely chained up or locked behind the property fence. If you do encounter an aggressive dog that is loose, be assertive, wave a stick at it, and as a last resort throw a few stones in its general direction. More likely than not, the dog will turn and run.

Snakes – A total of eight species of snake can be found in the Algarve. The three venomous species are 'back-fanged', making their bites largely ineffective against humans. Nevertheless, you should never attempt to handle any snake that you come across.

Cattle – In a number of places, you are likely to encounter cattle grazing freely. Give bulls and cows with calves a wide berth, and be prepared to step aside and allow animals to pass by quietly.

River crossings – Following heavy winter rains, normally placid streams can become raging torrents for short periods of time. Do not put yourself at risk by attempting to ford rivers in flood.

Hunting – Licensed hunting is permitted in many parts of the Algarve, particularly between November and February. Hunting activities should not disrupt use of the Via Algarviana, but it is a good idea to listen out for the sound of gunfire.

Fire – Wildfires have devastated large areas of forest in the Algarve in recent years. In hot, dry conditions, forest fires are a continual concern, though the period of highest risk – July and August – is outside the main walking season. Do not add to the problem by building fires or smoking in countryside areas. If you should spot a fire, call 117 to report it. Do not put yourself at risk by walking into areas affected by fire.

Accommodation

There is accommodation available at the end of every day's walking along the Via Algarviana. By British standards, rates are very cheap, and they usually include breakfast. Additional services, such as an evening meal, may also be available on request. Details of what's available can be found in the information at the start of each day section (I have not included establishments with minimum stay requirements or anything located an inconvenient distance from the trail). The standard of accommodation is generally very high.

In many towns and villages, there may be no more than one accommodation provider, so it is worth booking ahead to ensure availability. Apps such as Booking.com are extremely useful in allowing you to book accommodation in advance, but many smaller providers have no web presence at all and can only be contacted by telephone. This can present a problem if you don't speak Portuguese, so it's worth enlisting the help of local tourist information offices when arranging accommodation (a list of useful contacts can be found in the downloadable guide on the official website). If you haven't booked accommodation in advance, you can also ask guest house owners to ring ahead to arrange your next night's stay.

There are very few designated campsites either on or near the route of the Via Algarviana. Wild camping is a legal grey area, but you shouldn't have any trouble finding somewhere quiet and out of the way to camp (though be aware that the ground in the Algarve can be very hard and stony). In fact, if you haven't booked accommodation beforehand, it's probably worth taking a tent just in case.

Money

The currency of Portugal is the euro, which in summer 2015 was around two-thirds to three-quarters of the value of a British pound but has since fallen. Many smaller businesses in Portugal will only accept payments in cash, so it's important to carry a sufficient supply of euros when walking the Via Algarviana. If you do run out of money, there are banks in most towns in the Algarve, though these are open on weekdays only and may not have an ATM located outside. The availability of banks and ATMs in particular areas is given within the walk descriptions.

Language

The language of the Algarve is Portuguese, which has a reputation for being one of the harder European languages to learn. Many accommodation providers will speak a second, third, or even fourth language, but in many inland areas of the Algarve – particularly towards the east of the region – these will rarely include English. Here the most popular second languages are Spanish, German, and French, reflecting the popularity of the Via Algarviana among European hikers. Further west, where the Via Algarviana runs closer to the coast, English is much more widely spoken due to the predominance of English-speaking tourists in the coastal resorts. Nevertheless, most ordinary people you encounter will speak Portuguese only, and it is worth learning a few key words or phrases to help you get by.

Food and drink

Food and drink can be purchased at the end of every section of the Via Algarviana, though on the first two sections of the trail it may not be possible to buy a full evening meal. On most sections of the walk, you will also pass through villages where there are further opportunities to buy food and drink. The location of bars and restaurants en route is provided at the start of each day section. I have also provided information on the availability of grocery stores and public water fountains.

Businesses selling food and drink tend to fall into three main categories: grocery stores, cafe bars, and restaurants. Most cafe bars you pass will be small, unpretentious establishments serving a mainly local clientele. They may only provide a small range of snacks, but are always likely to serve bottled beer, wine, soft drinks, coffee, and water. On a hot day, it is always worth stopping to enjoy a bottle of the local Sagres beer in the shade. Restaurants are larger establishments, serving meals as well as drinks, though they will also function as bars for local people. In our experience, the food tended to be nicer (as well as cheaper) in the more traditional establishments, away from the main tourist areas. Meals tend to be very meat-based, however, and vegetarians and vegans may struggle to find alternative options.

Most accommodation providers (though not all) include breakfast as part of their standard charge. This is not the cooked breakfast served in most British bed and breakfast establishments, but a lighter meal of bread and preserves complemented by yoghurt and fruit. Evening meals can also be arranged with some accommodation providers, even where the business is not attached to a restaurant. Access to cooking facilities and a refrigerator may also be possible.

The range of food available in local stores can be quite limited, though you should be able to find enough snacks and sandwich fillings to keep you going for a day or two. Stores in the Algarve sell fresh bread daily, though this does not keep well and is best enjoyed on the day of purchase. In hot weather, fizzy drinks such as Sumo are also worth buying to complement water supplies. You may be lucky enough to pass through a town or village on market day, when a wide variety of fresh fruit and vegetables will be available.

In a number of places, you will also pass specialist shops selling local produce such as honey and *medronho*, a traditional liqueur made from the fruit of the *medronho* or strawberry tree. There is a particularly good *medronho* shop in Monchique.

How to use this guide

This guide divides the Via Algarviana into viable day sections, each beginning and ending at a sensible location offering accommodation and food. With one exception, these correspond to the official sections outlined on the official website of the Via Algarviana (www.viaalgarviana.org).

It has not been my intention to replicate materials that can be downloaded free of charge from the official website, where you will find maps, a GPX file, and a downloadable PDF guide (this contains a great deal of useful information, particularly with regard to accommodation and other facilities, but no detailed description of the trail itself). These are all worth consulting before setting off on your trip, but be aware that the links to the section maps only work from the Portuguese side of the website! If you intend to follow the alternative finish to Cabo de São Vicente, you should also locate the corresponding section information on the Rota Vicentina website (en.rotavicentina.com).

What this guide does contain is a clear and detailed description of the trail itself, together with a list of useful background information for each section: start and finishing points, distance, total ascent and descent, the time to allow, types of terrain covered, refreshments available, and accommodation options. Contact details for most can be found online or in the official guide. I have only mentioned facilities where these are located at a reasonable walking distance from the main trail and, in the case of accommodation, do not possess a minimum stay requirement. The official guide takes a more comprehensive approach, and you will find a number of facilities listed there which are not mentioned here.

My main priority while writing this guide has been to provide accurate and useful information of practical benefit to those planning to walk the Via Algarviana. Nevertheless, I also hope that this book is of interest in itself. Each section therefore contains a small amount of further information regarding places of interest you will pass along the way. Photographs taken by my partner and walking companion Tracy Burton on route can be found on Pinterest. We hope these will inspire you to put on your sun hat and hiking boots and head for the Algarve!

For photographs visit www.pinterest.co.uk/thewalkerswife

The Via Algarviana (GR13)

Waymarking

The trail described in this guide – including the alternative finish – is clearly waymarked. Nevertheless, before setting off it is worth noting the different types of markings used on each category of trail. This will avoid confusion in places where the Via Algarviana intersects with other promoted routes.

In Portugal as elsewhere in Europe, an official long-distance path is designated a *Grande Rota* or 'GR' and given an identifying number. Thus, the Via Algarviana is the GR13, the Rota Vicentina is the GR11, and the Grande Rota do Guadiana, which can be used as an alternative start for the walk, is the GR15. These numbers are used on official signposts, which also provide distances to relevant places along the route.

The Via Algarviana is also complemented by five waymarked link routes – confusingly, also marked GR13 – which connect the main trail with accessible population centres along the Algarve coast. Further information on these can be found on the official website of the Via Algarviana (www.viaalgarviana.org); the link to Aljezur and the Rota Vicentina (GR11) is described in this guide as part of the alternative finish.

Most waymarks you encounter will consist of variations on a simple red-and-white mark, and these follow the same pattern on every *Grande Rota*. A white horizontal bar over a red horizontal bar indicates the correct route; the two bars in the shape of a cross indicate a path or track that is not the correct route; while left and right turns are shown by a white horizontal bar above a right-angled red bar in the shape of an arrow.

The same pattern is found on shorter, local walks which have been designated a *Pequena Rota* or 'PR', except that the colours of the bars marking these trails are red over yellow instead of white over red. Where a GR trail and PR trail share the same path or track, markers consist of three horizontal bars: white at the top, red in the middle, and yellow at the bottom. The route of the Via Algarviana is complemented by several PR trails, allowing walkers to spend more time exploring a particular area if they wish (more information on the region's PR routes can again be found on the official website at www.viaalgarviana.org).

The alternative finish to Cabo de São Vicente follows a section of undulating clifftop path known as the Trilho dos Pesadores or Fishermen's Trail. This is marked using similar principles but in green and blue.

Accessing the Via Algarviana

Whether you intend to walk all of the Via Algarviana or just part of it, the best way to access the trail by public transport is via the regional train service from Faro (timetables on www.algarvebus.info). Opportunities to join the trail are particularly good to the west of the city, with waymarked link routes starting from the railway stations in Loulé, Mexilhoeira Grande, and Lagos; it is also possible to access the main trail from Silves. Heading east, the railway ends at the border town of Vila Real de Santo António. You will need to catch a bus from here to reach the start of the trail in Alcoutim, but unfortunately the service is rather infrequent (you can study the possible options on www.algarvebus.info). For this reason, you may prefer to begin your walk from Vila Real and use two linking trails – the Grande Rota do Guadiana (GR15) and the Ladeiras do Pontal (PR2 ACT) – to access the Via Algarviana in Balurcos. (You can follow the GR15 all the way to Alcoutim if you wish to walk the first section of the Via Algarviana as well.)

If you have flown into the Algarve and are travelling by train from Faro, you will also need to decide how you intend to make your way from the airport to the railway station. A bus service connects the airport terminal with the city centre (€2.22 fare in 2015), but this is not particularly frequent, and you may have to wait for an hour or more at certain times of the day or week (timetables at www.algarvebus.info). If you decide to catch a taxi into the city instead, the fare should come to around €10.

Alternatively, it's perfectly possible to walk into Faro from the airport – a distance of around 5km. To do so, turn right on leaving the terminal towards a roundabout. Bear right at the roundabout, then turn immediately left on to Rua Henriques Fernandes Serrao. This is initially a dirt road but later becomes surfaced. Keep straight ahead for about 1.7km, until the road bears right into Rua António Aleixo. With a level crossing ahead, turn right on to a track running alongside the railway line. The track is part of the Ecovia do Algarve, a long-distance cycle trail across the Algarve. Simply follow the railway as far as the station, where it's possible to cross to the main platform and ticket office.

If the above sounds too complicated, you can, of course, choose to catch a taxi direct from the airport to the Via Algarviana (this is more economical if there is a group of you), or it may be the case that the hotel where you are spending your first night can arrange for a transfer at a reasonable rate.

Leaving the trail presents less of a challenge. From Cabo de São Vicente, it's possible to catch a bus direct to Lagos if you reach the cape before 15:05 on a weekday. Otherwise, you will need to follow the road and cycle track for some 6km along the coast into Sagres and catch a bus from there (timetables can again be viewed on www.algarvebus.info). From Lagos, it's a slow but straightforward rail journey back to Faro.

For photographs visit www.pinterest.co.uk/thewalkerswife

Distances

1. Alcoutim to Balurcos: 24km
2. Balurcos to Furnazinhas: 14km
3. Furnazinhas to Vaqueiros: 21km
4. Vaqueiros to Cachopo: 15km
5. Cachopo to Barranco do Velho: 30km
6. Barranco do Velho to Salir: 16km
7. Salir to Alte: 19km
8. Alte to Messines: 20km
9. Messines to Silves: 30km
10. Silves to Monchique: 31km
11. Monchique to Marmelete: 16km
12. Marmelete to Barão de São Jão: 37km
13. Barão de São Jão to Vila do Bispo: 24km
14. Vila do Bispo to Cabo de São Vicente: 17km

Alternative finish via Aljezur and the Rota Vicentina (GR11)

12. Marmelete to Aljezur: 19km
13. Aljezur to Arrifana: 12km
14. Arrifana to Carrapateira: 24km
15. Carrapateira to Vila do Bispo: 22km
16. Vila do Bispo to Cabo de São Vicente: 14km

Day 1: Alcoutim to Balurcos

Day one of the Via Algarviana follows a convoluted route, initially heading north along the green, fertile valley of the Guadiana river. After leaving the river, the Via Algarviana climbs steeply west, passing through Corte Pereiras and on to the famous Lavajo menhirs. The trail then turns back to the south, crossing the Cadovais river and joining a long, steady climb up to Corte Tabelião. More undulating tracks lead up to the section finish in Balurcos.

Start: The quay in Alcoutim
Finish: Junction with the N122 road in Balurcos do Baixo
Distance: 24km
Total ascent: 610m
Total descent: 420m
Time: 7hrs
Terrain: A fertile river valley and then undulating scrubby hills. The trail follows mainly good-quality tracks, though there are also some shorter sections of road walking.
Refreshments: There are a number of bars and restaurants in Alcoutim, as well as a small general store. Along the trail, there are cafes in Corte Pereiras and water fountains in Corte Tabelião and Torneiro. There is a bar in Balurcos, but no restaurant at present. Evening meals may be available at the Casa do Vale das Horta (if ordered in advance), or alternatively you can follow the N122 north for just over a kilometre to the Restaurante O Bacelar.
Accommodation: There is accommodation available at the Guadiana River Hotel, the Pousada de Quietude (youth hostel) and Alcoutim Castle. Highly recommended is Los Molinos, just across

the river in Sanlúcar. Bed and breakfast accommodation at the end of the section can be found at the Casa do Vale das Hortas.

Walk instructions

1. From the information board by the quay, walk up the cobbled street towards the centre of Alcoutim and take the narrow street to the right of the Capela de Santo António (St Anthony's Chapel). A small general store to the right of St Anthony's Chapel is a good place to stock up on food for the day. Climb along a narrow, cobbled street to a small square, the Praça da República. Keep ahead through the square, then take the main cobbled street bearing right. At a junction, keep ahead along a two-lane tarmac road to cross a bridge over the Ribeira de Cadavais ('Cabo de S. Vicente a 300km').

2. After passing a parking area, take the next road on the right, the Avenida de Espanha. Follow the road to its end, just past the Guadiana River Hotel. Take a signed path up steps to the left and follow a narrow stony path up to a road. Turn right, following a Via Algarviana sign for Balurcos.

3. Just past the Pousada de Juventude (youth hostel), the road becomes a wide gravel track cruising gently above the Rio Guadiana. Where the main track forks, take the lower, right-hand trail descending gently towards the river ('Balurcos'). As the track forks again, shortly after a concrete hut on the right, turn left, away from the river. After a little over 50 metres, the track climbs back to the right. Follow it round another right-hand bend, ignoring a smaller track on the left. Curve left to continue up the Guadiana valley.

4. Where you reach a clear fork in the track, bear left and join a long, steady climb away from the river. Shortly after the track levels off, ignore a rougher track climbing ahead and continue along the main track, which bears right. The track climbs again,

passing through scrub-covered hills. Glancing back as you climb, you will be able to see the Rio Guadiana and the hilltop castle of Sanlúcar in Spain. Eventually, crest the brow of the hill and follow the track down to a junction with a two-lane road. Ahead of you is the village of Corte Pereiras.

5. Turn right at the road, passing the entrance gate to a house ('Herdade Monte Sol'). At a Via Algarviana sign a short distance beyond, turn right on to a small grassy track. This bears left, away from the house, and reaches a fork. Take the right-hand track (i.e. not the one up to the farm on the left) and continue to a tarmac lane. Turn left, entering the village, and shortly reach a junction by the Café Tempero.

6. Turn right and continue to crossroads. Take the road to the right, then fork left on to a stony track where the road bears right. The track turns left then climbs to the right. Rejoin a tarmac road and reach a junction. Turn left and follow the road out of the village.

7. Shortly reach a junction with another road. Cross straight over on to gravel track signed to Menires do Lavajo (the Menhirs of Lavajo). Follow the main track to an obvious fork. Take the left-hand track signed to the menhirs, shortly passing a path to the stones on the right. Continue along the track towards the village of Afonso Vicente.

8. At a fork just below the village, take the main, left-hand track continuing straight ahead. Climb to a junction and turn left. Take the next track to the right, keeping straight across a junction towards old stone walls. A concrete path continues between the walls to a lane. Turn left and, where the tarmac ends, take the track bearing right. Leaving the village, follow the track through rough fields and scrub to a junction with a two-lane road.

9. Turn right at the road and then immediately left on to another waymarked track. Descend gently to a fork and bear left. The track dips, climbs, then drops to a cross junction of tracks. Turn left and

descend into a valley, climbing back out to reach another cross junction of tracks. Turn right, the track eventually descending to cross the Ribeira de Cadavais – like many rivers in the Algarve, barely more than a trickle during the long hot summer months. A long, steady climb out of the river valley is followed by a gentle descent. Meet a road near the small village of Corte Tabelião.

10. Turn left towards the village. Pass the first few houses, then turn right on to a concrete track by an information board. Enter a small square with a water fountain and pass to the right of a shrine. At a second information board, keep ahead on to a grassy track and descend to cross a small river in a valley.

11. After crossing the river, climb steadily for some time, doubling back on yourself to the left. After cresting the hill, descend to cross another small stream and climb again. As you approach the village of Corte de Seda, ignore a smaller track continuing straight ahead and follow the main, waymarked track to the right. After a right-hand bend, fork left on to a smaller, grassy track following a drystone wall in the direction of the village.

12. Turn left at a road and keep straight ahead through the centre of the village. After passing round a right-hand bend, look for a sign directing you left, then immediately turn right past a community noticeboard. Follow the road out of the village to a junction with a two-lane road.

13. Keep straight across the road to continue along a waymarked track. After 300 metres, turn sharply right on to another track and follow this to a T-junction. This time turn left and continue towards the village of Torneiro. After a right-hand bend, the track becomes concrete and climbs steadily towards the village centre.

14. At the top of the hill, the Via Algarviana joins a local walking route, the PR2. Turn right, following a sign for Balurcos, and continue to a wide concrete square. Bear left here, ignoring a tarmac road heading right and keeping ahead along a concrete

track past more houses. Just past the final house, where the concrete surface ends, take the middle of three tracks ahead (the one with a stone wall to its immediate right). Keep ahead along the track until you emerge on the main road in Balurcos. The Casa do Vale das Hortas (bed and breakfast accommodation) is a short distance down the road to the right.

Highlights

Alcoutim

The town of Alcoutim is situated on the right bank of the Rio Guadiana, directly opposite the Spanish village of Sanlúcar de Guadiana. There is evidence of Greek, Roman and even Phoenician settlement in the area, and in the eighth century the Moors built a hilltop fortress just to the north of today's town. With the incorporation of the Algarve into Portugal in the thirteenth century, settlers were encouraged to move to Alcoutim to prevent Castilian incursions and to assert Portuguese control over the lucrative river trade. The old Moorish castle was abandoned at this time and a new castle built on a hill overlooking the river and town.

The Rio Guadiana

With a length of over 800km, the Guadiana river is one of the longest rivers on the Iberian Peninsula. The lower course of the river is navigable for some 68km and has been an important trade route connecting inland Spain and Portugal with the coast for millennia. Rich alluvial soils either side of the river provide a fertile corridor for farming, creating a green ribbon through an otherwise arid landscape.

Menires do Lavajo

The Lavajo menhirs are a group of prehistoric standing stones dating from the late Neolithic or Chalcolithic period (*c.* 3500–

2800BC). The group consists of three carved menhirs, the largest of which is over three metres in height; all three have been decoratively carved with circles and other symbolic elements. In common with other prehistoric megaliths, the precise function of the Lavajo menhirs is unclear, but their alignment suggests some kind of religious purpose, the stones perhaps demarcating a particular sacred space.

For photographs visit www.pinterest.co.uk/thewalkerswife

Day 2: Balurcos to Furnazinhas

The second section of the Via Algarviana is far shorter than the first. From Balurcos, undulating tracks wind through a delightful rural landscape to Palmeira then down to the banks of the Foupana river. This is a beautiful spot and a great place for a rest, but be aware that the river may not be safe to cross following heavy rain. Beyond the river, the trail climbs steeply to Corte Velha before crossing further gently rolling hills to Furnazinhas.

Start: Junction with the N122 road in Balurcos do Baixo

Finish: In the centre of Furnazinhas, near the Casa do Lavrador

Distance: 14km

Total ascent: 330m

Total descent: 349m

Time: 4hrs

Terrain: Undulating tracks through rolling hills, with one potentially tricky river crossing (the Ribeira da Foupana). Steep climb from the river to Corte Velha.

Refreshments: There are cafe bars in Corte Velha ('Ti Emídio') and at the end of the section in Furnazinhas. Water is available in Palmeira. Evening meals are available from the Casa do Lavrador.

Accommodation: Bed and breakfast is available from the Casa do Lavrador in Furnazinhas.

Walk instructions

1. From the crossroads in Balurcos, head straight over the main road and into the village. At crossroads a short distance before the former Snack Bar Poço Velho, bear left on to a track between stone

walls (not the road to the immediate left of this). On reaching a junction in a more open area, turn right and climb gently to a junction with a road. Turn right again, but this time bear immediately left to continue along the main tarmac lane. As you walk along the lane, you will be able to look back across the village of Balurcos, now below you to the right.

2. At a sharp right-hand bend, a local museum ('Museu') is signed back towards the village. However, the main route bears left, on to a gravel track heading away from Balurcos. At the next track junction, bear left again. Ignore a track to the right and keep straight ahead towards the main IC27 road. Keep straight across a junction of tracks a short distance ahead, and join a tarmac lane passing below the main road. Turn left straight after the tunnel, on to a lane running parallel to this road.

3. The tarmac reverts to gravel a short distance after the lane starts to bear right, away from the main road. Continue ahead along a wide stony track, ignoring a number of tracks turning off to the left. The track then passes round a left-hand bend – ignore the smaller track continuing straight ahead – and starts to descend. Curve right at the bottom of the hill, still following the main gravel track. Wind gently through open wooded hills until a fork of two clear tracks is reached.

4. Take the left-hand track heading downhill and continue to a cross junction of tracks. Take the level track to the left, which shortly bears right and descends steeply towards Palmeira. At a fork by the first houses, bear right, passing a bench and water fountain. Bear left to descend along a tarmac lane towards the main, lower part of the village at the bottom of the valley.

5. At the bottom of the hill, cross a (dry) stream bed and turn immediately right on to a track along the valley. Ignore a track forking to the right across the stream, and instead bear left, back towards the main IC27 road crossed earlier. Cross the stream bed

(note the stone pillars for use in times of flood) and join a tarmac lane heading up to a bridge over the main road. Once across the bridge, the tarmac soon reverts to gravel. Climb away from the main road in a roughly south-easterly direction.

6. At a junction of tracks at the top of the climb, bear right and start to descend back towards the main road. Once again, the track crosses the road, this time passing beneath it where it is carried across the valley by a viaduct. Continue ahead, the Ribeira da Foupana now visible in the deep valley to your left. The track soon begins to drop towards the river, eventually reaching a junction near the valley floor. Following a waymark, bear right and immediately cross the bed of a side stream. Continue up the banks of the main river to a waymark post just before the ruins of a former mill.

7. Follow the sign left, in the direction of the river, then bear right across a stony flood beach. Turn left towards an obvious crossing point, stones providing a dry passage across the river in normal conditions (after heavy winter rains, it may be difficult to cross the Ribeira da Foupana safely). There is initially no obvious path on the far side. Bear right and follow the river upstream across stony, scrubby ground until you emerge on a clearer track. Continue across another stony area until you reach a clear track climbing steeply to the left.

8. Join this track and begin a long, steep climb out of the valley. You will pass through a forest of holm oak, a large evergreen oak native to Mediterranean regions. The gradient eventually eases, though there are still two more sections of ascent before the climb finally ends. Soon after, drop to a junction with a two-lane road and turn right. The village of Corte Velha is shortly visible ahead.

9. As the main road curves right, keep straight ahead on to a smaller road into Corte Velha. The road heads straight through the

centre of the village then bends right to pass in front of a small cafe bar. Re-emerge on a two-lane road and turn left.

10. Follow the road round a left-hand bend. At a second left-hand bend a short distance ahead, keep straight ahead on to a track and continue to a cross junction. Turn left, descending initially then climbing. Follow the main track as far as a fork in front of a small utilities hut. Bear right (the left-hand track drops to a two-lane road and roundabout) and continue towards Furnazinhas, a ruined windmill to your right.

11. The track ends by a larger utilities building. Join a stepped cobbled path dropping down to the village, bearing left by a smaller building to drop to a junction with a cobbled road. Turn right, passing in front of the house you were just above. Take the next cobbled street on the left and descend to where the road forks either side of a wall. Join the street to the right and follow it round a left-hand bend between buildings. Emerge on a two-lane tarmac road and turn right. A short distance ahead, a signed cobbled lane on the left leads to the Casa do Lavrador. If you continue past this point, you will reach a small square in the centre of the village containing a cafe bar and a Via Algarviana information board.

Highlights

Ribeira da Foupana

With a permanent flow, the Ribeira da Foupana provides an oasis for wildlife during hot arid conditions. The banks of the stream attract numerous species of plant, including ash, willow and oleander, while forests of holm oak cloak the valley slopes. The river has a tendency to flood following heavy winter rains, and crossing at such times may be impossible or dangerous.

Furnazinhas

Furnazinhas is a sleepy inland village where it is still possible to see traditional handicrafts being practised such as basket weaving and mat making (from the fibres of esparto grass and palm leaves). There is no restaurant here – only a cafe bar – so you will need to make arrangements with the Casa do Lavrador for an evening meal to be provided. Two signed circular walking routes – the PR9 and the PR10 – also start and finish in the village, should you wish to spend an extra day exploring the area.

For photographs visit www.pinterest.co.uk/thewalkerswife

Day 3: Furnazinhas to Vaqueiros

The Via Algarviana continues through a landscape of rolling hills, scrubby trees and rock rose. There are a number of hamlets and small villages along the route, but many of these – such as Monte Novo – have been largely abandoned. The largest settlement passed through, Malfrades, is still inhabited and possesses a public shelter and water fountain. Approaching Vaqueiros, walkers will need to decide whether to continue into the village or make the 2km detour to the Cova dos Mouros mining park.

Start: In the centre of Furnazinhas, near the Casa do Lavrador
Finish: The centre of Vaqueiros, near the Casa de Pasto Teixeira
Distance: 21km
Total ascent: 389m
Total descent: 327m
Time: 6hrs
Terrain: Undulating but good-quality tracks through scrub-covered hills. There is a small amount of road walking.
Refreshments: Water is available in Malfrades and at the end of the section in Vaqueiros. There are two restaurants in Vaqueiros: the Casa de Pasto Teixeira and the Casa de Pasto Domingos. Groceries can also be bought from the latter.
Accommodation: Accommodation is available at the Cova dos Mouros mining park, a few kilometres north of Vaqueiros, or at the Casas D'Aldeia – run by the owners of the Casa de Pasto Teixeira restaurant – in Vaqueiros itself.

Walking instructions

1. From the Casa do Lavrador, return to the main village road and turn left. Just before an information board in the centre of the village, turn right up a cobbled street (the one passing directly in front of a cafe bar). As you approach the top of the village, the track bears left and shortly turns to gravel. At a signed junction at the top of the hill, take the track bearing left and descend gently to a junction with a road.

2. Turn right, shortly following the road round a left-hand bend. Soon after, take the next track on the right ('Preguiças') and follow this as far as a clear fork just beyond a left-hand bend. Ignore the track heading steeply uphill to the right, and instead take the lower, left-hand track, which descends gently to a waymarked fork. Follow the sign for the Via Algarviana, which continues along a track curving gently downhill to the left. The track then winds its way through a valley, a usually dry stream bed below to the left. After crossing the stream, climb gently to a junction with a track.

3. Turn sharply left, back down towards the valley. The track drops to cross the stream again then climbs. At a fork, continue on the main track as it bears left round a bend, still climbing. Ignore any smaller tracks to the left or right, and climb towards the village of Monte Novo. At a clear fork where the track levels off slightly, take the flatter track bearing left towards the village.

4. As you enter Monte Novo, keep straight ahead across a junction of tracks then follow the main gravel track bearing right. Emerge at a junction of roads and keep straight across ('Preguiças'). Where a track crosses your route, leave the road to the right and wind gently downhill into a valley. At a cross junction, take the track to the left, heading slightly uphill into pine woods, and continue through a wooded valley. Look out for a smaller waymarked track on the right, which takes you across the valley. Climbing out of the

valley, keep ahead at a cross track and past another track on the left. Not far beyond this, reach a clear two-way fork.

5. Take the lower, left-hand track, which curves slightly to the left. At the next clear fork, follow the upper, left-hand track, then continue ahead along a clear track for more than a kilometre, passing through scrubby pine woods and ignoring any tracks to the left or right. After a lake comes into view on the right, the track bears left and the village of Monte das Preguiças can be seen ahead. In a dip below the village as you leave the forest, take the track curving left. At the next cross track, turn right, passing an old stone well, and climb towards the village between drystone walls.

6. Join the main village road, which bears left at the top of the village. Keep ahead past a lane on the right and join a concrete track. This shortly exits the village and reaches a junction with a road. Turn left and climb gently to the hamlet of Balurcinos.

7. At the first houses, turn sharply right on to a track signed to Malfrades and Vaqueiros. At a fork, take the track curving left, then shortly pass a well on a right-hand bend. Straight after, keep ahead at a cross track, then follow a level section of track through a lovely meadow. After crossing a ditch, the track forks again. Keep straight ahead (the left-hand track), then take a track curving right at the next junction. Crest a small hill, keeping ahead past a track on the left. Cross the brow of another hill – there are wind turbines visible ahead – and drop to a fork. Take the level track curving right, then reach another fork within sight of Malfrades. Keep ahead towards the village (the right-hand fork) and drop into a dip. When joined by another track from the right, curve left towards the village.

8. Join a concrete track at the edge of the village and pass round a sharp right-hand bend. Straight after, turn sharp left to continue up through the centre of the village. At a split in the track, bear left, then turn sharply to the right, uphill between whitewashed houses.

Almost immediately, the track forks again. Turn left this time, and follow the track round a right-hand bend to emerge on a road by a community noticeboard, a water fountain, and a shelter with benches.

9. Turn left and shortly reach a junction with a larger two-lane road. Keep ahead, following a Via Algarviana sign for Vaqueiros. After a right-hand bend, fork left on to a track and then left again where the track divides soon afterwards. The track winds its way along a valley, passing through an open barrier between fences. Below on the left is a small stream. After crossing the stream, the track climbs towards electricity wires, a small pool visible below to the right. Keep ahead at a cross track, cresting the hill soon after. Descend gently, still heading towards the wires, and at the bottom of the hill cross a bridge over a small river.

10. Keep straight ahead along the main track up the hill. The track levels out, passing through another barrier between fences and continuing towards the electricity wires seen earlier. Just before reaching them, the track curves left and runs parallel to the wires. Climbing again, it bears right to continue directly below the wires before eventually passing under them. At this point, reach a fork.

11. Bear right, away from the wires, on to a level track. Continue ahead, ignoring any tracks to the left or right. After a brief, gentle descent, the track levels off once more and Vaqueiros comes into view in the valley on the left. In the next dip, reach a junction with accommodation signed to the right ('Alomojento'). To reach this, you will need to follow the track for some 2km to the right to the Cova dos Mouros mining park.

12. To continue on the main route, turn left and descend towards Vaqueiros. Join a concrete track as you approach the village, descending to cross a stream then climbing up to a road (there is an information board just to the left of this junction). Turn right then immediately left, heading up into the village. The Casa de Pasto

Teixeira (accommodation and restaurant) is on your left-hand side, a short distance past the first road on the left.

Highlight

Cova dos Mouros

As well as accommodation, the Cova dos Mouros mining park also offers visitors the chance to explore the long history of copper mining in the area. A waymarked trail leads past mining remains dating back some 4,500 years, to the beginning of the Chalcolithic period, while reconstructed settlements and tools provide a glimpse of what life for these pioneer miners might have been like.

For photographs visit www.pinterest.co.uk/thewalkerswife

Day 4: Vaqueiros to Cachopo

Between Vaqueiros and Cachopo, the Via Algarviana crosses steep, undulating terrain dominated by cistus and stone pine plantations. However, there are also a number of hamlets – Monchique, Amoreira and Casas Baixas – where it is still possible to see small working farms surrounded by kitchen gardens and small agricultural plots. Indeed, one of the highlights of the section is the traditional rural architecture encountered. A final climb through a beautiful cork oak forest leads up to Cachopo.

Start: The centre of Vaqueiros, near the Casa de Pasto Teixeira
Finish: The Restaurante Retiro dos Caçadores in Cachopo
Distance: 15km
Total ascent: 543m
Total descent: 410m
Time: 4hrs
Terrain: Good-quality gravel tracks on the whole, but also a fair amount of climbing and descending.
Refreshments: Groceries are available at the start and end of the section. Evening meals can be bought in Cachopo at the Restaurante Retiro dos Caçadores and the Restaurante 'A Charrua.
Accommodation: Bed and breakfast accommodation is available at the Restaurante Retiro dos Caçadores. Bunkhouse accommodation is also available at the old elementary school in Casas Baixas.

Walk instructions

1. From the Casa de Pasto Teixeira, take the road bearing left above the restaurant. Turn left at the next opportunity, shortly emerging in the village square (if required, water is available from a fountain in front of the church). Turn right towards Taberno Angelino, then right again, heading uphill away from the square. Fork left in front of a large white house and continue climbing to the top of the village. At a waymark post, keep ahead on to a concrete track signed to Monchique and Cachopo.

2. Almost immediately, reach a fork. Take the track bearing slightly left, the concrete surface soon turning to gravel. Climb to another fork with local walking routes ('PR') signed in both directions. Take the left-hand track again and continue uphill. Just after passing a track on the left, you will crest the brow of the hill and be able to see wind turbines through a gap in the hills ahead. The track now winds gently down into a valley before climbing back out through pine woods. Continue climbing for some time, until you reach a clear two-way fork at the brow of the hill.

3. Take the track continuing straight ahead, towards Monchique. Just past a white building, the track curves right and up into the village. Join a concrete track, which passes round a left-hand bend and quickly reaches the western edge of the hamlet. Join a tarmac lane for a few metres, then keep straight ahead on to a gravel track signed to Cachopo. At the first fork in the track, bear left and follow a winding descent into a lovely valley. As you descend, ignore a track heading uphill to the right and continue down towards the valley floor.

4. Approaching the bottom of the hill, ignore a track to the left and curve slightly right along the valley. At the next fork, descend briefly to the right and then bear left to join the start of a long climb. The track briefly levels off then climbs sharply to the right.

This second climb is soon over and ends at a junction with another track. Turn left for a few metres, then take a track on the right heading down into a thickly wooded valley. The track climbs out of the valley then dips again, the village of Amoreira now visible ahead (not Casas Baixas as one sign suggests).

5. Where the track forks, take the grassy track on the right towards the village. This curves right and then left before entering the village and joining a concrete track. Keep ahead on this for a few yards and then turn right. You will soon reach a cross junction with a small white utilities building ahead. Turn right here, up the hill, then take the next gravel track on the left by a water storage tank. Leave the village and follow a winding, contouring track across piny slopes. At a fork, keep straight ahead along the main track, heading gently downhill.

6. At a waymarked junction of tracks near the bottom of the valley, take the track turning sharply right ('Cachopo'). This immediately curves back to the left and contours across the slope, a small river valley below to the left. Heading north, pass to the right of higher ground then curve left. Join a track coming out of the valley on your right and bear left again. The track drops to cross a stream then climbs out of the valley towards electricity wires. Pass below these and continue climbing to a waymarked junction of tracks.

7. Bear right here (effectively straight on) to continue along the main track. Almost immediately, another track joins from the right and you bear left, still climbing. Shortly reach the top of the hill, another set of electricity wires a short distance ahead. Beyond these is the village of Casas Baixas and in the distance wind turbines. Continue ahead towards the village.

8. Join a tarmac lane by a barn and bear right (effectively straight on). The lane climbs round a right-hand bend then levels off. Continue round a left-hand bend in the direction of the main village. At the edge of the village, follow the main lane round a

right-hand bend by municipal bins. (If you wish to explore the village, or are planning to stay overnight at the former elementary school, take the narrow street bearing left at the bins.) Shortly reach a left-hand bend by a board containing information about Casas Baixas and the local walks available. Follow the road left ('Cachopo') and continue as far as the next track on the right, also signed for Cachopo.

9. Join this track and climb along a valley. Views open out ahead at the crest of the hill. After another small rise, follow the main track curving left. At a fork with pine trees ahead, bear left to continue along the main track. Drop into a valley, passing cultivated plots to your right. Climb out of the valley, keeping straight ahead uphill at a cross track. The track shortly crests the hill then winds its way down through another beautiful valley. Follow this along, ignoring tracks climbing to the right and left, then drop to cross a small watercourse.

10. Once across the ford, turn immediately left. Follow the valley along, the stream to your left separating the track from a number of agricultural plots. After starting to climb, take the main track curving right by a white agricultural building. The track now runs along the side of another valley, slightly up the slope with fertile plots below to the right. In hot weather, cork oak trees lining the track provide welcome shade.

11. Reach a cross track as Cachopo comes into view and turn left. Shortly join another track dropping from the left and continue ahead on to a concrete track. Climb to a junction with a two-lane road, where you will find a Via Algarviana information board. Turn right towards a roundabout, and then bear left, up into the village. The Restaurante Retiro dos Caçadores is on the left-hand side of the road a short distance ahead.

Highlight

Casas Baixas

Casa Baixas illustrates some of the challenges – as well as possible solutions – facing inland villages in the Algarve. Once the centre of a thriving rural economy, the village is now only home to around twenty residents, all over fifty. Many traditional architectural features – whitewashed walls, cattle enclosures, and community ovens – have been preserved intact, relics of a bygone age. To boost local tourism, the former village school has been converted into a 'Centro de Descoberta do Mundo Rural' (Rural World Discovery Centre) providing basic accommodation along with a kitchen and outside eating area. Visitors can access three circular local walking trails from the centre and a longer multi-day trail (the GR23) connecting Casa Baixas with two other rural centres in Mealha and Feiteira. For more information visit www.in-loco.pt

For photographs visit www.pinterest.co.uk/thewalkerswife

Day 5: Cachopo to Barranco do Velho

The section between Cachopo and Barranco do Velho passes through the heart of the forested Serra do Caldeirão and contains some of the most spectacular scenery in the eastern Algarve. However, it is also one of the most demanding sections of the Via Algarviana, with numerous climbs and descents and a long final ascent to Barranco do Velho. Some walkers may therefore prefer to split the section in two, stopping overnight at the rural centre in Feiteira (see below for details).

Start: The Restaurante Retiro dos Caçadores in Cachopo

Finish: A Tia Bia (restaurant and guest house) in Barranco do Velho

Distance: 30km

Total ascent: 1,280m

Total descent: 1,160m

Time: 8hrs

Terrain: Mainly good-quality tracks, though with lots of ups and downs! There are a few fords to negotiate, and care is required on a couple of short, awkward descents across loose gravel.

Refreshments: Groceries can be bought at the start of the section in Cachopo. There is one snack bar en route, in Parises. There are water taps in Castelão and Parises, and a restaurant – A Tia Bia – at the end of the section.

Accommodation: Bed and breakfast is available at A Tia Bia at the end of the section. It is also possible to split the section in two and spend a night at the Centro de Descoberta (Discovery Centre) in Feiteira.

Walking instructions

1. Turn left just before the Restaurante Retiro dos Caçadores on to Rua 1 Maio. After a slight rise, bear left up a cobbled track with a paved strip down the middle. Pass a general store – Mercearia Eduarda – and emerge in a square by the parish church. Bear right, then immediately turn left to pass to the right of the church (there are public toilets outside the church if required). At the back of the building, turn right down Rua da Igreja. Continue to the end of the road, then bear right down a narrow concrete path. Drop to a junction with a cobbled track and bear left to continue downhill. Turn left again, and re-emerge on the main two-lane road through Cachopo.

2. Cross the road to a waymark post and continue down a cobbled track to a public wash house. Bear left, using concrete pillars to cross a wet, marshy area. Rejoin a cobbled track and bear right up the hill.

3. Emerge on a road by a water tap and turn left. Where the road curves left a short distance ahead, keep straight across to a gravel track signed to Barranco do Velho and Currais. Head gently uphill between trees. Where a track forks off to the left, keep straight ahead, climbing more steeply.

4. At the top of this steep section, join another track and turn right. The track continues uphill, but less steeply. Pass two tracks on the left, views opening up to a hill with wind turbines on it. Carry on up the main track, reaching a junction shortly after the track levels off. Turn left and go past a track on your immediate right. Continue up the small rise ahead and then along a ridge, the village of Currais in the valley to your right.

5. At a junction of tracks, turn right and descend towards the village, shortly joining a lane between houses. You are likely to pass lots of barking dogs on the descent into Currais – all safely

chained up. Bear right at the bottom of the hill to continue along the main village road, which wiggles its way along the bottom of the valley. Turn left on to a concrete track and start climbing out of the valley. As you leave the village, keep straight ahead on to a wide gravel track and climb steadily.

6. At a cross junction of tracks, keep ahead between two pillars, following a road sign for Alcaria Alta. (In many rural areas, gravel tracks still form the main routes between villages and may be signed for vehicles as well as walkers.) To your left are steeply descending valley slopes containing numerous planted terraces. Take the lower, left-hand track at a fork and descend gently. Continue to descend along the main track, winding down through several curves into the valley.

7. Cross a stream at the bottom of the valley and climb past an intriguing castellated house. Follow a long, winding climb out of the valley along the main track. After the gradient eases, the track contours its way around the hill and the hamlet of Alcaria Alta becomes visible higher up the slope. After swinging right, the track climbs again, levelling off after a left-hand bend. Keep ahead and climb for a final time to reach a junction. Alcaria Alta – no more than a small group of houses – is to your left at this junction.

8. The Via Algarviana continues along the level track to the right. At the next fork, bear right again, following a road sign for Feiteira. Stick to the main track, ignoring turn-offs to the right and left. Initially, the track heads gently downhill, in a roughly west-south-west direction, but soon levels off along the line of a ridge. Eventually, it begins to descend again, at a point where a house can be seen across the valley to the right. Continue round a left-hand bend and into a eucalyptus grove. Emerging from the trees, you will shortly reach a junction and waymark post. At this point, you have the option of shortening the section by turning right and following the signed route to Feiteira.

9. To continue on the main route, take the track to the left signed to Castelão and Barranco do Velho. (In 2015, the signpost at this junction indicated a distance to Barranco of 15.5km – it's actually at least another 20km to the section end.) At a cross track, keep straight ahead on to a rougher, more steeply descending track. As it descends, the track turns left and quickly reaches a fork. Turn sharply right and follow a steep winding descent into a valley.

10. At a junction near the bottom of the valley, turn left and descend for a few metres more to cross a stream bed. The track then begins a long, steep climb back out of the valley, eventually reaching a T-junction with a track contouring across the slope. Turn right, the track shortly beginning to climb again. At a junction just past the brow of the hill, follow the main track to the right, a valley now below you to the left. Keep ahead past a fork on the right and climb a small rise to a junction with a concrete road. The alternative route via Feiteira rejoins the main route at this point.

11. Turn left, following the road down the hill into Castelão. Fork left in the houses, continuing downhill. Shortly after passing a bench, take the track descending to the left. After a few metres, turn right, following a road sign for Barranco do Velho. Leaving the village, descend along a wide gravel track into a valley. Keep right at a fork (effectively straight ahead) to continue on the main track and drop to a concrete bridge over the Ribeira de Odeleite.

12. Immediately after the bridge, take the track on the right signed to Parises. This is a narrower, rougher track, obviously little used by vehicles. The track climbs along the valley, providing lovely views over the river below. After a brief descent into a side valley, the track climbs again, this time through cork trees, and bears left, away from the river. Parises comes into view as you emerge from the valley, the gradient easing off for a while. After a final pull through cork woodland, turn left at a junction, heading straight up towards houses, and emerge on a two-lane road near picnic tables.

Signed to the left is the Centro de Interpretação da Rota da Cortiça (Cork Route Interpretation Centre).

13. Unless visiting the cork centre, follow the road to the right. Turn right at crossroads a short distance ahead, on to a minor road signed to Barranco do Velho. (For the waymarked link route to São Brás de Alportel – also numbered as GR13 but not described in this guide – turn left at the crossroads instead of right.) You will immediately pass a small snack bar. Bear left at a fork in the road, and shortly reach another fork by a water tap. Bear left again and descend to a third fork by a stone cross. This time bear right and join a gravel track heading down into a valley. Keep straight ahead at a cross track and continue downhill to a rougher, stonier section of track at the bottom of the valley.

14. At a fork in the track, bear left (a ford across the Ribeira de Odeleite is visible a short distance along the right-hand track). Climb as far as a left-hand bend, then gently descend to cross a small stream. The track continues up the valley, the stream now concealed to your left by thick vegetation. At a fork, follow the main track round a right-hand bend. Some 200 metres further on, at a second fork, take the lower, left-hand track. This continues up the valley, at first climbing steadily and then more steeply. Leaving the valley, the track climbs to the right through pines and emerges on a ridge. Keeping left, follow the ridge uphill to a T-junction of tracks.

15. Turn right, following a Via Algarviana sign for Barranco do Velho, and immediately begin to descend. Bear left at a fork ('Montes Novos'), and follow the main track through pine woods. Pass round a right-hand bend, then to the left of a pond, and continue up the slope ahead. After cresting the rise, the track descends steeply into a valley. At a clear fork near the bottom, bear left on to a waymarked track and descend for a few awkward metres over loose gravel to a stream.

16. Cross the stream, using the concrete pillars to the side if the river is in flood. The track immediately curves left and climbs steeply. As it curves back to the right, the track levels off and approaches another ford (the Ribeira de Odeleite again). Do not cross the stream this time, but turn sharply left on to a smaller track just before it. Climb steadily through meadows to meet another track and bear left. A few metres ahead, take a steep, stony track to the right and begin a demanding climb through a mix of pine and eucalyptus woods. Near the top of the climb, join another track and bear left, then climb again to reach another junction. Bear left again and curve left along the crest of a ridge.

17. Stay with the main track as it turns sharply to the right and drops into a dip. Ignore the track climbing ahead and turn sharply left to continue downhill. Where the track appears to end, climb across an awkward stony slope on the right towards a waymark post, then turn sharp left down another awkward slope to cross a stream. From here, join a clear track climbing to the left. Still climbing, pass round a sharp right-hand bend and shortly enter more eucalyptus and pine woods. Joining another track, bear right and continue along the crest of a ridge to an offset cross track. Bear right and climb again until you reach a fire lookout tower. Go past this and drop right to a junction in a dip. Ignore the walk signed to the left and continue ahead, climbing slightly. Emerge in a car park by a community centre. Nearby, you will find an information board about the country park you have just entered, the Parque Temático da Serra do Caldeirão.

18. Keep ahead, passing to the right of the car park, and bear right to reach a junction with a two-lane road. Turn left and follow the road to a big white building, the Casa da Cantoneiros ('house of the road menders'). Just past the building is an information board about Barranco do Velho. Turn left here and follow a track gently downhill through pine woods. After passing Fonte do Chafariz

('the Chafariz fountain'), the woodland track turns uphill to the left. Emerge on a concrete track and drop right to a junction with a two-lane road. If open, there is a small handicraft shop selling local products (including *medronho*) downhill to the left in Barranco do Velho. To reach the end of the section, turn uphill to the right, in the direction of a Via Algarviana sign for Salir. After a left-hand bend, you will arrive at A Tia Bia, a hotel, restaurant and cafe bar on the right-hand side of the road.

Alternative route via Feiteira

The alternative route via Feiteira follows sections of two circular trails: the GR23 to Feiteira and the PR4 from Feiteira to rejoin the Via Algarviana in Castelão. We have not attempted to walk this route, so cannot provide a detailed description, but the relevant maps and further information can be found at www.in-loco.pt/pt/percursos-pedestres

Highlights

Cork

With its extensive areas of dense cork oak forest, the Serra do Caldeirão is one of the most important cork-producing regions in the Algarve. Harvesting the cork entails stripping the thick, rugged bark from the trunks of trees using a small axe. The process does not harm the tree, which grows a new layer of bark and is ready to harvest again after another nine to twelve years. The cork forms the basis for a variety of products, including stoppers for wine bottles and as a tough, well-insulated flooring. As a native tree species, cork oak forests also support a diverse ecosystem and were one of the last known habitats of the Iberian lynx in Portugal.

Barranco do Velho

Barranco do Velho is a small village situated high up on the southern edge of the Serra do Caldeirão. The surrounding area is one of the wettest in the Algarve, second only to Monchique in the amount of annual rainfall it receives, and is famous for its historic wells, springs and fountains. Barranco is also well known for the quality of its local *medronho*, a traditional liqueur made from the fruit of the arbutus or strawberry tree, which is sold in the small handicraft shop in the village.

For photographs visit www.pinterest.co.uk/thewalkerswife

Day 6: Barranco do Velho to Salir (Casa da Mãe)

The section begins with a beautiful upland walk along the Serra do Caldeirão's southern escarpment. There are lovely wild flower meadows and extensive views – including a first glimpse of the coast. A long forestry descent leads to a ford across the Rio Seco and an abrupt change in the character of the landscape as the Via Algarviana enters the Algarve's *barrocal*: the fertile agricultural region between the narrow coastal strip and the hilly uplands of the *serra*. Roads, tracks and meandering orchard paths take the trail into Salir.

Start: A Tia Bia (restaurant and guest house) in Barranco do Velho

Finish: The parish church in Salir (for the Casa da Mãe)

Distance: 16km

Total ascent: 269m

Total descent: 526m

Time: 5hrs

Terrain: Mainly gravel vehicle tracks, with a long descent off the *serra* into the *barrocal* region east of Salir. A ford across the Rio Seco may present problems after heavy rain. Remainder of route is on a mix of tracks, quiet roads and rural paths.

Refreshments: Nothing en route, though there are number of cafe bars and small shops as you enter Salir. Evening meals are available from the Restaurante Porto Doce and the Papagaio Dourado. A supermarket (Jafers) can be found at the southern end of town, on Rua Manuel Dourado Eusébio.

Accommodation: Bed and breakfast is available from the Casa da Mãe, a short distance to the north of Salir. Alternative accommodation can be found about halfway through the section at the Quinta do Coração. There may be a campsite at Alagoas, a few kilometres to the east of Salir, but it hasn't been possible to verify this.

Walking instructions

1. Leaving A Tia Bia, turn right on to the main road signed to Lisboa (not the side road immediately adjacent to the car park). As you leave the village over the crest of a hill, turn left on to a gravel track and then bear immediately right past an information board for the Barranco do Velho Biodiversity Station (the track is also signed to Salir). Follow a lovely level track across open scrubland, the sea now visible in the distance for the first time on the trail. The track runs through a nature reserve and passes several information boards about the plants and animals that can be seen.

2. On reaching a T-junction with another track, turn left. At the next fork, bear right (not the PR route to the left) and continue along the crest of a ridge. After a short, steep rise and descent, reach a clear fork and take the left-hand track continuing straight up the hill ahead. The track continues to undulate, eventually reaching a fork where a track drops down to a road on the right.

3. Ignore the track to the right and keep straight ahead. Bearing left, continue along the ridge towards the distinctive shape of a former windmill – Eira de Agosto. Keep straight ahead at a cross track, then climb slightly to the right. Pass the windmill and continue ahead along the ridge. At the next fork, where the track splits either side of a tree, bear left. The track continues along the ridge, passing to the left of a meadow and then dropping steeply to a wide gravel area adjacent to a road.

4. Take the track on the left ('Salir') and descend easily through dense cork woodland. At a fork following a slight rise, bear right and start to descend again, this time more steeply. The track eventually levels off near a concrete hut, then rises slightly and drops to a junction with another track at the bottom of a valley. The route continues down the valley to the left, in the direction of a road sign for the N124. (Turning right will take you up to the Quinta do Coração, a rural bed and breakfast set in idyllic surroundings.)

5. About 200 metres down the valley, look out for a smaller, stonier track forking right (the bottom section of the track looks like it may flood after heavy rain). Climb steadily out of the valley through a mix of scrub and pine. At the top of a rise, ignore a track climbing steeply uphill to the left and continue ahead along the main track, which now starts to descend gently along the left-hand side of a valley. At the next fork, take the track bearing left into a wooded valley. Before long, you will be able to spot Salir on a hill over to the right. Continue ahead until you reach a fork by a triangle of scrubby grass.

6. Bear right at the fork and then immediately left on to a stony track alongside a small river – the Rio Seco. Within 20 metres or so, drop right and cross the river via a makeshift causeway. The far bank of the Rio Seco makes a great picnic spot, and there is a nice bathing pool above the ford. Follow the track up to a T-junction and turn left. A few metres ahead is another junction, with a local PR route signed to the right. Ignore this and keep straight ahead on to a more prominent vehicle track. Pass between meadows and shortly reach a villa. Just past this is another track junction by houses. Bear left towards a two-lane road.

7. Turn left then immediately right, on to a smaller road signed to Salir. Follow the road round a left-hand bend (a picnic area and campsite are signed to the right) and descend into a valley. Climb

as far as another left-hand bend, then fork right on to a track signed to Salir. (The waymarked link route to Loulé continues straight ahead up the road.) Climb steadily along this narrow, stony track until you emerge back on the road. Turn right and enjoy easy level walking as far as a sharp left-hand bend by an information board about dry fruit orchards.

8. Leave the road by keeping straight ahead on to a good-quality gravel track. At a fork, keep straight ahead again on to a smaller track between drystone walls. Emerge on a narrow concrete track by houses and turn sharply right. Take the lower, right-hand track at a fork ('Fujanca'), and continue until you reach a narrow, waymarked path on the left. Bear left at a fork and follow a single-file path gently uphill through meadows. Continue ahead along a shady route between walls to emerge on a vehicle track. Keep straight ahead down the hill.

9. At a sharp left-hand bend, continue ahead down a loose stony path. (The initial few metres are slightly awkward; for a less difficult descent, follow the track round the corner and turn back on yourself.) A single-file path leads down into a valley then follows a short, steep climb up to a level track. Turn right for about 100 metres. As the track starts to drop slightly below trees, turn left on to a shady, single-file path and climb up to a concrete track by derelict buildings. Keep ahead between these and then turn immediately right on to an easily missed path to the left of a high wall (the path may be overgrown in places).

10. Emerge on a gravel track and turn left. Turn right at a cross track and descend along a concrete track towards Salir. At a road, turn left, still heading towards the village. At the next road junction, bear right, following a sign for 'Centro'. (To reach the Jafers supermarket, turn left ('Loulé') and then right at the next T-junction.) Go past a narrow lane on the right, then bear right up a cobbled passage signed 'Igreja Matriz' (parish church). Climb steps

to the church, then bear left towards Largo Bar. There are fabulous views from the tower to the right of the church, and a welcome rest can be enjoyed on one of the nearby benches.

11. If staying at the Casa da Mãe, it is now necessary to leave the Via Algarviana by turning right on to the Rua da Igreja. Curve right, descending below the church, then look for a concrete track forking left. Descend steeply to a junction with a road and turn left. Cross straight over a larger, two-lane road and continue ahead towards the satellite village of Ameijoara. The Casa da Mãe is on your right as you reach the first group of houses.

Quickest route to restaurants from the Casa da Mãe

If walking into Salir for an evening meal, turn left out of the Casa da Mãe, then take the next track on the right, just before a house. Follow the track round a left-hand bend, then continue ahead to a junction with a two-lane road. Keep straight ahead on to a road opposite signed to the castle and climb to an offset crossroads. Keep ahead on to Rua José Silva Elias and arrive at a T-junction opposite the Restaurante Porto Doce. Salir's other restaurant, the Papagaio Dourado, is a short distance to the right.

Highlights

Dry fruit orchards

Dry fruit orchards – figs, almonds, olives and carobs – are a characteristic feature of the Algarve *barrocal* and were once a mainstay of the local rural economy. Their fruits are termed 'dry' because the trees they grow on require little or no watering but derive all the moisture they need from rain and dew. Sections of the Via Algarviana utilize part of a historic network of sunken pathways routed between the orchards' limestone boundary walls.

Salir

Salir is an attractive town of narrow streets and low, white houses. There are a range of facilities, including restaurants, cash machines and a supermarket. The town grew up around a Moorish castle during the Almohad period (12th and 13th centuries) before being taken over by invading Portuguese forces under Paio Peres Correira (d.1275). One theory regarding the town's name is that it derives from the Arabic word for 'escape', called out by the town's Muslim defenders as they fled in panic. The castle ruins are attached to the town museum and are worth a visit.

For photographs visit www.pinterest.co.uk/thewalkerswife

Day 7: Salir (Casa da Mãe) to Alte (Alte Hotel)

The section begins with a pleasant stroll through a rich agricultural landscape, passing through a number of small villages and hamlets. Dirt tracks then lead towards the Cerro do Vieira and the start of a steep climb on to the hill. After a pleasant ridgetop walk and descent into Benafim, the Via Algarviana heads north, through several dry fruit orchards, before eventually entering Alte alongside a beautiful stream. A final steep climb from the village leads to the Alte Hotel.

Start: The parish church in Salir

Finish: The Alte Hotel above the village of Alte

Distance: 19km

Total ascent: 408m

Total descent: 340m

Time: 5hrs

Terrain: Mainly good-quality tracks and quiet roads. However, a section of the route after Calçada may be muddy after rain and is followed by a steep, stony climb on to the Cerro do Vieira.

Refreshments: The Restaurante Hamburgo is just off the main route in Benafim. Alte contains a wide range of bars, cafes, stores and restaurants, and meals are also available from the Restaurante 'A Cataplana' in the Alte Hotel.

Accommodation: Bed and breakfast is available from the Alte Hotel (just past the village of Alte). There is a one-bedroom self-catering property, Alte em Férias, in Alte itself, while accommodation can also be found at the Quinta do Freixo, a large working farm between Benafim and Alte.

Walking instructions

1. From the Casa da Mãe, retrace your steps to the top of Rua da Igreja and turn right. Follow a narrow street down through the historic centre of Salir. At the bottom of the hill, and immediately before a road on the right signed to Salir's castle, turn left, on to Rua José Silva Elias. (Before leaving Salir, it is worth climbing up to castle ruins, which can be accessed via the local museum, the Pólo Museológico de Salir.)

2. Reach a T-junction opposite the Restaurante Porto Doce and turn right. Immediately pass another restaurant, the Papagaio Dourado, and turn left down the road alongside it. Take the next road on the left and drop to a junction with a busier two-way road, where you will find an information board about the next section of the Via Algarviana to Alte.

3. Turn right and follow the main road past a department store and cafe. Just beyond a zebra crossing, take a concrete track on the left signed to Benafim and Alte. This descends gently then levels out. Ignore a local walking route forking right and shortly begin to descend again. Follow the track round a sharp right-hand bend and then sharply left to continue downhill. Go round another left-hand bend and follow a level track towards gates marked 'Propriedade Privada' (private property). Just before the gates, follow the track sharply right and cross a bridge over a river.

4. After crossing the river, continue along a level concrete track through cultivated fields. You will pass a number of waterwheels and an information board. Near a house, the Casa da Fonte, you will come across another information board about a local walking route – part of the Rota da Água – linking many of the area's traditional wells, waterwheels and irrigation channels. Just past the

house, bear right and immediately reach a crossroads. Keep ahead, following road signs for Beirada and Almarginho, and climb gently uphill through the latter.

5. Shortly after a right-hand bend, the lane forks by a tree growing in an enclosed concrete circle; take the slightly smaller road climbing to the left. As you leave the village, the gradient eases, and the road continues gently uphill through a mix of woods and fields. Straight after a derelict building, take a lane forking left and continue past a house on to a gravel track. After several hundred metres of pleasant level walking, the track bears right and climbs to a junction with a road in the village of Serro de Cima.

6. Turn left and follow the road up through the village. As you start to head gently downhill, ignore a lane turning sharp right and continue ahead on to a concrete track. Follow this to the village of Calçada and back on to a tarmac road. As you approach the far end of the village, look out for a waymarked track on the left (this is just past an orchard and before more houses begin on the left). The track curves sharply back to the left, descending gently. Where a smaller track continues straight ahead along the top of a meadow, stick to the main track, which bears right and descends to a cross junction of tracks. Keep straight ahead downhill along a gravel track.

7. The next section is quite complicated – and may also be muddy. After the track levels off, look out for a dirt track on the right with a waymark painted on to a rock a short distance along it (if you reach a fork in the gravel track, you've gone about 50 metres too far). Bear left where the track forks, then bear left again at another fork to reach a junction with a more defined track. Cross straight over this and turn immediately right on to a narrow, overgrown path below trees with a stone wall to your left. Follow this along until it emerges back on to the main dirt track. Keep straight ahead up the hill, climbing steeply through scrub to the top of a ridge.

8. On meeting a stone-based track, turn right along the top of the ridge. The track soon turns to dirt again, with scrub blocking views to either side. Initially, the track follows the crest of the ridge, but soon drops slightly below and to the right of it. As you start to descend towards Benafim, the track becomes enclosed by a stone wall and fence protecting orange plantations. Pass round a sharp right-hand bend and a sharp left-hand bend. Join a road on the outskirts of Benafim and descend gently to a T-junction opposite a vivid yellow house.

9. Turn right and follow the road up to a roundabout. Turn left, then take the next road on the right ('Rua de Sá Carneiro'), following a Via Algarviana sign for Alte. After a short climb, continue on to a narrow, cobbled street. Keep ahead at a junction with a tarmac road, shortly following the road round a right-hand bend. Take the next left – towards a 'Stop' sign at a junction with a larger road. Keep straight across on to a cobbled lane, which climbs to the right. At a junction of cobbled roads, turn left, in the direction of the parish church. Follow the cobbled street past the church and community centre and back out on to a tarmac road.

10. As the road starts to descend, turn right on to a narrow, enclosed track between stone walls ('Azinhaga Dahazas'). (For the Restaurante Hamburgo, keep ahead, then follow the next road on the left down to a junction with a main road.) Follow the track up the hill to emerge on the corner of a tarmac lane. Bear left on to the road, following a sign for Alte. After passing a farm access track on the right, the lane starts to descend. Bear right at a fork, and continue downhill along a gravel track towards a house and lake.

11. As you approach the valley floor, ignore a smaller track forking right and instead follow the main track round a sharp left-hand bend. Ahead is a ford, which can be bypassed via stepping stones to the left. (Immediately after the ford, a track on the right leads to the Quinta do Freixo – the house and lake visible earlier – where

accommodation is available if required.) The track now climbs diagonally left up the valley slope. At the top of the climb, continue on to a gently descending tarmac lane.

12. Where you are joined by another lane from the left, turn right and rejoin a track. After a level section, the track starts to descend gently again. Where another track joins from the left, bear right and continue down to the bottom of the valley. Quite suddenly, you will emerge on a cobbled road by a kiosk and cafe bar (closed on Mondays). Continue ahead, alongside a stream and picnic areas, and follow the cobbled road gently uphill to the edge of Alte. As you approach the village, you will pass public toilets.

13. Keep ahead up Alte's main cobbled street. At a fork by a small general store, head uphill to the right, following a sign for 'Centro'. Where the street levels off and starts to bear left, keep ahead up a narrow, cobbled passage ('Rua dos Pisadoiros'). (Alternatively, continue along the village's main street for bars, restaurants, the parish church, and a supermarket.)

14. Continue straight ahead at crossroads. At the top of the hill, turn right on to a tarmac road and bear immediately left. Follow the road up the hill, continuing once more on to cobbles. Shortly after the street becomes tarmac, reach a junction with a level, wider road. Turn right on to this and then immediately left up a concrete track. After the last house, continue on to a gravel track, which climbs initially then levels off as more houses appear on the left. The rear gates of the Alte Hotel are numbered 16, and the hotel staff will open these for you if you ring ahead. Alternatively, you can make your way round to the main entrance by taking a pathway on the left about 80 metres beyond the gates.

Highlights

Wells and waterwheels

Waterwheels were first used to extract water from wells or cisterns in the Algarve during the Moorish occupation – a practice which greatly expanded the area of land available for agriculture. Using this complex hydraulic mechanism, water could be extracted from underground sources and distributed to orchards and cultivated fields via a series of gravity-fed irrigation channels. Traditional technologies of this kind are particularly prevalent around Salir and form the basis for a short circular walk.

Alte

The pretty village of Alte is a great place to unwind and be a tourist for the day. Entering the village from the east, you will pass the springs or *fontes* for which the village is most famous – a picturesque area ideal for picnicking. The village itself is one of the most unspoilt in the Algarve, with whitewashed houses, traditional chimneys, and narrow cobbled alleyways. Not to be missed is the famous Alte waterfall, which can be accessed from the large roundabout to the south-west of the main village (take the road to the right of the cemetery then join a track descending into the valley).

For photographs visit www.pinterest.co.uk/thewalkerswife

Day 8: Alte to São Bartolomeu de Messines

From the Alte Hotel, the Via Algarviana passes through a cultivated landscape of farms, small villages and dry fruit orchards. The path is often narrow, bringing additional variety and interest to the walk. After a long, steady descent down the scenic Barranco do Vale, the trail veers south, through Portela, before turning back north towards São Bartolomeu de Messines. The highlight of this final stretch is a narrow path along the lush riverine valley of the Meirinho.

Start: The Alte Hotel above the village of Alte
Finish: The parish church in São Bartolomeu de Messines
Distance: 20km
Total ascent: 302m
Total descent: 443m
Time: 5hrs
Terrain: A varied but not too difficult section comprising roads, tracks and narrow trails. A busy main road is followed for a short distance towards the end of the section.
Refreshments: There is a garage shop in Portela but nothing else until the Restaurante 'Ti Raquel', a short distance before the end of the section. São Bartolomeu de Messines contains a wide range of shops, cafes, restaurants and bars.
Accommodation: Bed and breakfast accommodation is available from Bartholomeu Guesthouse in the centre of town, while budget hostel accommodation can be found at the Hostel Casa do Povo de Messines. There are also two smaller establishments offering

rooms: the Pensão Guia on Rua Heróis de Mucaba and the Pensão/Café Martins on Rua José Rodrigues Martins. Just outside São Bartolomeu de Messines, in Monte de São José, is the Residencial 'Ti Raquel'.

Walking instructions

1. From the rear of the Alte Hotel, continue along the track, which passes more properties before dropping to a two-lane road (this is the road climbing up from Alte past the front of the hotel). Turn right for a little under 50 metres, then take the next road on the left, signed for Torre and S. B. Messines. Follow the road round a right-hand bend, then look out for a grassy/dirt track forking downhill to the right. Take this and continue on to a path winding downhill between stone walls. Ignore a clear path climbing back up to the road on the left, and keep ahead between the walls to rejoin the road further along. (The final section of path may be overgrown, and it might be preferable to rejoin the road earlier.) Bear right and continue to a crossroads.

2. Keep ahead on to a dead-end road signed to Alcaria do João. Before long, bear right on to a gravel track and head gently downhill. Where the track descends sharply to the right, keep ahead on to single-file path (look for a marker on a tree). The path drops to the right, crossing a narrow, stony stream bed, then bears left along the top edge of an orchard. Pass through an enclosed section below trees, then continue along a ledge path above a steep drop to the left. The path climbs to the right then levels off. At an apparent fork, take the lower path to the left (look for the red-and-white waymarks). Eventually, climb right, up steps formed by boulders, to a junction with a dirt track.

3. Turn right here, heading roughly north-east. Continue as far as a junction with another track, then climb to the left. After a left-hand bend, the track levels off and turns back towards the west. Enter

the village of Torre and climb along a concrete road between houses. At a junction, turn left, then curve right to reach another junction. The concrete surface is now replaced by tarmac. Turn right and then immediately left on to a concrete track just before the wooden toy workshop of Da Torre. The track drops to the right then curves right again to reach a T-junction with a road.

4. Follow the road to the left until you reach a sign indicating the beginning of Terça. Immediately after the sign, turn right on to a gravel track signed to S. B. Messines. Follow the track through a semi-rural landscape of rich, cultivated plots. The track climbs towards houses and joins a road. Keep ahead to a junction at the crest of the hill, and again keep straight ahead. Drop gently downhill to rejoin a gravel track, and continue past orange groves and orchards in the direction of three distant wind turbines. Pass a house at the top of a climb and immediately reach a fork in the track.

5. Take the track to the left and descend gently. São Bartolomeu de Messines is now clearly visible ahead, but the route into town is very convoluted so there's still plenty of walking left to do. The track continues gently downhill along a pleasant valley, passing a number of properties before eventually curving right and turning to tarmac. Climb to a junction with a two-lane road and turn left.

6. After a little over 200 metres, look out for a gravel track on the left heading up past a ruined house on a hill. Once past the ruin, the track winds its way gently downhill towards a motorway viaduct spanning the valley. Pass to the right of a pond and then a goat farm. At a cross track immediately after the farm, keep ahead towards the motorway and shortly reach a fork to the left of a small lake. Stick to the main track (the right-hand fork), which continues to head gently downhill towards the motorway viaduct. At a junction about 100 metres before the viaduct, take the left-hand track, which runs roughly parallel to the motorway on your right.

Climb to a junction with a two-lane road and turn left, past a garage and shop.

7. About 130 metres up the road, turn right at a Via Algarviana sign for Portela and S. B. Messines. Climb along a road, then keep to the left of a house ahead. Follow a gravel track up to Portela, then take a lane in the village heading downhill to the left. This shortly curves right, passing between derelict houses to reach a junction with a slighter larger road. Turn right and follow this road through the village to its far end. Continue on to a gravel track.

8. With a fence ahead, bear left and descend alongside the motorway, which is once again to your right. At a junction with a road, turn right and pass below the motorway. Once through the tunnel, fork right and then immediately left. Follow a gravel track ahead through scrubland until you reach a fork by a drystone wall. Turn sharply left so as to continue with the wall on your right. The track now heads gently downhill, a number of large polytunnels visible to your left. Stick to the main track, which curves left and then right past a large garage-type structure. Emerge on the corner of a road.

9. Turn right and follow the road below a large main road and then round left- and right-hand bends. Fork right at a junction up to a large concrete building. Keep ahead, passing to the right of the building, and join a gravel track. Follow this gently downhill past a number of properties. After a left-hand bend, reach a junction with a tarmac lane and turn right.

10. About 1km after joining the lane, and 50 metres or so after crossing a stream, take a cobbled track forking right. About 100 metres up the track, fork right where indicated on to a single-file path descending diagonally across a valley slope. Take the lower, right-hand path at a fork and descend again, zigzagging down to a wooden boardwalk and handrail. Follow the path below trees and along the banks of a stream – the Ribeiro Meirinho. Cross a

wooden footbridge to the left of a dam and continue up a lovely wooded valley. Eventually emerge on a wider path and turn sharply left. Climb diagonally back across the valley slope to reach a large orange building (a fruit depot) on top of the hill. Keep ahead along the wall and then bear right at an access road.

11. Reach a T-junction and turn right on to a busy main road – by far the most unpleasant stretch of road walking along the Via Algarviana. After around 650 metres, and 50 metres or so after a house on the right, escape the traffic by turning left on to a lane. This climbs, curving left, then levels off as it passes houses. Turn right at a crossroads. At the next junction, bear right and then immediately left, continuing with orange groves to your right. Enter a built-up area (Monte de São José) and reach a junction with a main road (the Restaurante/Residencial 'Ti Raquel' is a short distance to the right).

12. Follow the road to the left for a little over 100 metres. As you approach a sign indicating a roundabout ahead, bear left on to a lane towards a church. Just past the church, turn right and descend along a steep cobbled track. At the bottom of the slope, keep ahead towards the main road then join a track bearing left. This runs alongside a railway and below a bridge carrying the main road. Straight after the bridge, where the track curves right towards a car wash, keep ahead along a single-file path. This descends awkwardly down a slippery bank to a road and information board. Keep ahead to a T-junction and turn left.

13. Follow the road into the centre of São Bartolomeu de Messines and down the town's main shopping street (the Pensão Guia and Pensão Martins are on streets to the left of this). Keep ahead on to a narrow street towards the church and shortly reach a junction and 'Stop' sign. Bartholomeu Guesthouse is on your immediate right; the Hostel Casa do Povo de Messines can be reached by reached by following instructions for the start of the next section.

Highlights

Ribeiro Meirinho

The lush riverine valley of the Meirinho is a pleasant surprise on the approach to São Bartolomeu de Messines. Trees growing alongside the river include the dwarf fan palm, the only native species of palm to be found in Europe.

São Bartolomeu de Messines

São Bartolomeu de Messines is a busy market town with all the associated facilities. The most interesting part of the town lies behind the parish church, where historic cobbled streets wind between low, whitewashed housing. Adjacent to the church is the Museu João de Deus, which houses a collection of materials relating to the eponymous 19th-century poet. Born in the town in 1830, João de Deus is widely recognized as being one of the greatest Portuguese poets of his generation.

For photographs visit www.pinterest.co.uk/thewalkerswife

Day 9: São Bartolomeu de Messines to Silves

From São Bartolomeu de Messines, the Via Algarviana continues across an undulating landscape of farms, fields and orchards to Pedreiras. The wooded valley of the Rio Arade, dominated by a large reservoir trapped behind the Barragem do Funcho, marks a sudden change in the landscape. After crossing the dam, the trail climbs steeply into the hills – without doubt, the toughest part of the day's walking. Wooded trails then head south towards Silves and a final road walk into town.

Start: The parish church in São Bartolomeu de Messines
Finish: Silves
Distance: 30km
Total ascent: 1,020m
Total descent: 1,130m
Time: 8hrs
Terrain: Mostly good-quality vehicle tracks, with some road walking at the beginning and end of the section. After a level walk around the reservoir above the Barragem do Funcho, there is a long, strenuous climb into the hills above the Arade valley.
Refreshments: After leaving São Bartolomeu de Messines, there are no refreshments or drinking water available until Silves – be sure to carry enough food and liquid for the day. There are numerous stores, restaurants and bars in Silves.
Accommodation: There are plenty of places to stay in Silves – see Booking.com for details.

Walking instructions

1. From the centre of São Bartolomeu de Messines, walk up the steps to the parish church and bear left, towards the front of the building. Drop down more steps to return to the road and keep ahead towards a Via Algarviana waymark post. Follow the indicated direction up a narrow, cobbled road to the right. After passing below an arch, turn left along another cobbled street. Continue ahead along a narrow, mainly level road until further progress is blocked by industrial buildings. Drop left for a short distance to return to the town's main street.

2. Follow the main street to the right for just under 200 metres. Just after the Hostel Casa do Povo, where the main road bears slightly left, fork right up a smaller road, the Rua do Furadouro. Continue along this road for about 500 metres, to where a waymarked concrete track on the left drops to a railway and pedestrian crossing. Turn left on the far side of the railway and then immediately right, on to a road signed to Furadouro. Within a few metres, turn right again and begin to climb.

3. Take the next road on the left, which follows a level route out of São Bartolomeu de Messines and along the edge of a cork forest. Where the larger road bears downhill to the left, keep ahead on to a smaller lane. This climbs gently, passing more houses and cultivated fields. Where the tarmac ends, continue on to a grassy/dirt track. After passing a ruined farmhouse, this drops left and reaches a junction with a road.

4. Turn sharp right and follow the road across a flat valley floor before climbing to a crossroads in the hamlet of Pedreiras. Continue straight ahead, following a road sign for Vale Bravo, and climb out of the Messines valley along a steep, narrow lane. Pass round a right-hand bend by a house at the top of the hill, then turn downhill to the left along a gravel vehicle track.

5. At the bottom of the hill the track forks. Follow the right-hand fork uphill towards houses, passing between buildings. The track then winds its way gently downhill through a lovely valley, eventually levelling off near a cross track. Keep straight ahead and shortly join the shores of a long, narrow reservoir formed by the Arade river. Follow the clear winding track along the wooded shores of the reservoir for several kilometres. Eventually the track climbs to pass above houses and approaches a ruin. Curving left, climb steadily away from the lake until the track levels off below electricity wires. Continue ahead to emerge on the corner of a road near picnic benches.

6. Follow the road to the right for about 350 metres. At a Via Algarviana signpost, fork right on to a smaller road and descend steeply to a picnic site above the reservoir. Continue past gates preventing further access to vehicles and follow the road round to the left towards the Barragem do Funcho (Funcho dam). This is the upper of two major dams on the Arade river, the other being the Barragem do Arade, a few kilometres to the south. Cross the dam, then take the track forking left, down into the valley. With a large concrete building ahead, turn left to continue downhill.

7. Ahead of you a bridge crosses the river below the dam. Turn right before the bridge and follow a gravel track down the valley. Where the track widens and forks, bear right, away from the river, shortly reaching another fork where the track narrows. Bear right again, this time leaving the main track and heading up a side valley. The track climbs, winding its way up steadily through a narrow, enclosed valley. After you cross a small stream, the gradient steepens and a long haul follows before you reach a junction with a wider gravel cross track near the top of the valley. Turn left and climb again, passing round a number of twists and turns. Emerge on the crest of a ridge with extensive views down towards the Algarve coast.

8. Turn sharply right on to a smaller track. The track shortly hairpins left and heads gently downhill along the line of a ridge. The climbing is still not over, however, and there are a few more sharp undulations to tackle before the track levels off below eucalyptus trees. At a junction, bear left to continue along the main ridge track. After a slight rise, reach a clear fork. Bear left again, this time leaving the main track. Descend to a clear cross track in a wide gravel area and turn right to continue downhill. Descend into a thickly wooded valley and continue ahead.

9. At a fork, take the better track bearing right, then immediately fork right again on to a smaller, ascending track. Continue ahead on to a better track at the top of the hill, then fork right at the next junction and descend into a valley filled with dense eucalyptus woods. Follow the valley along, eventually leaving the woods and reaching a junction with another track. Bear left and continue down the valley until the track climbs gently to a fork.

10. Take the right-hand track, which continues to climb above the valley on the left. Before long, pass a ruin and drop back down towards the valley. The main track now climbs steeply ahead, but bear left before the climb on to a path running along the lower valley slopes. This eventually drops to join a track at the bottom of the valley. Continue ahead towards Enxerim (a village to the north of Silves), meeting a wider gravel track in front of a cultivated field and house.

11. Bear slightly right (effectively straight ahead). The track curves right, climbing past another house, then continues to wind its way past houses and cultivated fields. After a left-hand bend, the Via Algarviana continues to the right, along a wide, stony track; however, to access Silves, you will need to continue ahead along the main vehicle track to a junction with a road (there was no signpost in May 2015 to indicate where to leave the Via Algarviana for Silves).

12. Bear left at the road. After cresting a rise, descend to a junction below Castelo de Silves (Silves Castle) on the outskirts of town – there's a bar, the Pastelaria Castelo, just before the junction. Following signs for 'Centro', continue ahead up a cobbled road climbing to the left of the castle. Drop left at a fork (again signed for 'Centro') and descend below a wall to a T-junction. Turn right and follow the road into the centre of Silves.

Highlight

Silves

During the Moorish occupation, Silves was the most prominent city in the Algarve region, prospering to the point of being known as 'the Baghdad of the West'. At that time, the Rio Arade was navigable by large ships right up to Silves, which remained the case until the 19th century. The splendid castle built by the city's Moorish rulers – the largest in the Algarve – still dominates Silves and is undoubtedly the most impressive military structure to be built under Muslim rule in Portugal. There are plenty of other attractions worth visiting in Silves, including the municipal museum and cathedral, and it is worth incorporating a rest day into your schedule to explore the town fully.

For photographs visit www.pinterest.co.uk/thewalkerswife

Day 10: Silves to Monchique

From Silves, the Via Algarviana heads north across rolling forested hills dominated by pine, eucalyptus and cistus (rock rose). The terrain is steep and undulating, but extensive views can be enjoyed from the ridges. A long descent eventually leads to a ford and bridge across the Ribeira de Odelouca and the start of a long, meandering climb to the summit of Picota. The climb is tough, but the scenery is magnificent. The Via Algarviana then descends through dense cork oak woodland to Monchique.

Start: Silves

Finish: Tourist information centre, Monchique

Distance: 31km

Total ascent: 1,440m

Total descent: 980m

Time: 9hrs

Terrain: Undulating forestry tracks in the first half of the section are followed by a long climb – on a mix of tracks and narrower paths – to the summit of Picota (774m), then a shorter descent into Monchique. Several river crossings may be difficult after heavy rain. Watch out also for an area of bare rock around the summit of Picota which may be slippery when wet and present navigational difficulties in poor visibility.

Refreshments: There are no refreshments or drinking water available between Silves and Monchique. Given the length and difficulty of the stage, it is therefore essential that you carry enough food and liquid for the day. Monchique contains several bars and restaurants, as well as a supermarket.

Accommodation: The Quinta da Corte offers accommodation in an idyllic woodland setting high up on the slopes of Picota. In Monchique itself, the obvious place to stay is the rather old-fashioned Miradouro da Serra, close to the tourist information centre. Bica Boa, at the northern end of town, provides bed and breakfast accommodation with a more contemporary feel, while rooms can also be found at the Pensão Bela Vista and the Hospedaria Descansa Pernas.

Walking instructions

1. From Silves, retrace your steps to where you left the Via Algarviana previously and turn left on to the wide, stony track. Continue ahead, keeping a stream to your right until it cuts in front of you below a road bridge. Follow a waymark up the steep bank on your left to return to the road. (If rejoining the Via Algarviana from Silves, you can choose to continue along the road to this point.) Turn right and cross the bridge. Bear left immediately afterwards on to a track running parallel to the road. As the road the curves right, drop left to cross a stream.

2. There are a number of tracks ahead. Take the one to the left initially, then immediately turn right on to a track heading up a valley. At the next junction, leave the main track by joining a rougher track climbing steeply to the right. This twists right and left then joins the line of a ridge, the Enxerim valley and river now below to your right. Continue along an undulating track with a number of steep climbs.

3. Reach a wooden shelter at a junction of tracks and bear right. The track continues to undulate steeply. Keep right at a fork, descending initially. The track enters a eucalyptus forest and is joined in a dip by another track from the left. Go round a left-hand bend and reach a three-way fork. Take the track on the left, climbing briefly then descending easily to a right-hand bend.

Ignore a misleading private property sign across the track ahead; the path you want is just behind the chain and steeply down to the right. After a stony descent, emerge by a small lake.

4. Keep ahead along the track to the right of the lake, then turn sharp left to continue along the far shore. At the end of the lake, the track bears right, down into a grassy valley. Fork left at a junction, abandoned farms visible on the hill ahead. As you turn to the left, cross a small stream, then fork right towards the abandoned farms. Climb past the buildings and plunge back into eucalyptus forest. The track continues to climb steadily.

5. Reach a junction at the top of the climb with open views ahead. Turn right along a level track, which winds its way around the hill. Where continuing ahead would take you up a steep, smaller track, follow the main track as it turns sharply left downhill. Cross a dry stream bed at the bottom of the hill and bear right. Climb steadily to a junction with a track on the crest of a ridge, farm buildings visible across the valley ahead.

6. Turn right, then keep ahead on to a wider gravel track climbing from the houses in the valley. After being joined by another track from the left, there's a good view of Picota's summit ahead. The track now curves right, following the border of a meadow to a cross junction of tracks. Turn sharp left to continue with the meadow on your left and pine trees to the right. Pass to the right of a lake and keep ahead past a track leading to a house and farm buildings. At the next fork, take the main track heading downhill to the right and descend along a narrow valley.

7. Eventually, you will reach a track ahead marked with a dead-end sign. Stay with the main track, which bears right and climbs slightly. The track curves right and suddenly the mountains are once again in front of you. Join a surfaced road and immediately fork left down a narrow track into a valley. Cross the Odelouca river at a ford (this can be avoided by continuing along the road)

and follow the track below the road above. Rejoin the road a bit further along and follow it up to a T-junction.

8. Turn right and follow a two-lane road along the Odelouca's valley, the river below you to the right. After about 400 metres, look out for a waymark directing you over the crash barrier to your right and down a narrow path. After a brief descent, join a level grassy track and turn left. Follow a pleasant riverside trail through woods and meadows to a junction with a gravel track. Turn left along this and climb back up to the road.

9. Turn right, crossing a tributary of the Odelouca. The road climbs then gently descends. Just before the next climb, fork left on to a track dropping into a wooded valley. Follow a clear, shaded track up the valley, fording a stream (the Ribeira de Monchique) on three occasions. After crossing the stream for the third time, bear left on to a waymarked path. The path becomes narrow and stony, climbing across a slope then dropping to cross a small stream in the tree-shaded valley below. Continue up the valley to the right of the stream until level with a ruin on your right. This is part of a former spa complex – Fonte Santa – and contains a number of stone tanks filled by warm-water springs.

10. Cross the stream on your left (the path is not immediately apparent) and turn left along an overgrown path through bracken. The path soon climbs clear of the thick valley vegetation and winds its way uphill. After emerging on to open hillside, bear right and climb steeply for about 50 metres on a loose dirt track. At this point, look out for a path on the left. This follows an easier, zigzagging route, rejoining the dirt track higher up the slope. Follow a clear path/track crossing the slope to the left and emerge at a junction on a ridge.

11. Turn right and climb along the ridge. At a fork a short distance ahead, bear right on to a track climbing steadily across the slope. Where the track levels off, briefly descend towards an old farm

building. Meet a track in front of the building and turn left, continuing downhill. After a right-hand bend, the track levels off and continues through cork woods. Emerge on a two-lane road and turn up the hill to the right.

12. After about 180 metres, take the next road on the left ('Caldas de Monchique' and 'Fornalha'). Follow this road for about 50 metres, then fork right on to a rough track. Ignore the track continuing ahead towards a house and turn right, straight up the hill. Keep ahead past a level track on the left, the gradient shortly easing as the main track curves slightly left. Climb through eucalyptus trees and join a better, more level track shortly after passing below electricity wires.

13. Keep ahead across the slope. Pass above ruined farm buildings at the head of the valley and follow the main track uphill to the right. The track curves right again, winding its way across a wooded slope, then passes round a sharp left-hand bend. At a fork, turn right, back towards the electricity wires. Pass below the wires again and follow them across the slope. The track then turns back under them, climbing and curving to the right. After a left-hand bend, the summit of Picota can be seen about 2km to the west. A winding uphill track leads into cork woods and on to a surfaced lane. Pass a number of old farm buildings and continue to climb gently through beautiful mountain woodland.

14. Reach a track turning sharply left signed to Quinta da Corte. Follow this up towards the house until level with the terraced field on your left. At this point, look for a path forking away from the track to the right. Climb through woodland, keeping straight ahead at a fork. The path is not always clear in the woods, so look out for waymark posts. Emerge on a road and cross straight over on to a road opposite signed to Picota.

15. After about 100 metres, the road suddenly narrows. Join a gravel track on the level and climb through eucalyptus woods. At a

junction of tracks, where the views suddenly open out ahead, turn right and climb on to a ridge. At the next track junction, turn sharp right and then – within 50 metres or so – sharp left. You should now be heading gently downhill through more eucalyptus woods. A fence will appear on your right, and there are views across the Monchique valley below towards Fóia.

16. Meet a lane and climb steeply to the left. The trees open out along the ridge and the road turns to the right. Where the tarmac ends at an information board, keep ahead up a steep, sloping path to a beacon and lookout tower on the summit of Picota.

17. Use waymarks and cairns to help navigate your way down the mountain's rocky western slopes. Join a woodland path and continue ahead along the crest of a ridge, enjoying fabulous views of the Algarve coast. With denser woodland ahead, bear right at a junction of paths by a wooden signpost ('Monchique'). The path becomes a track and descends to a lane. Turn right, then bear left at a fork to continue downhill. The road shortly levels off. At the next fork, bear downhill to the left above a garden pagoda. The lane passes round a sharp left-hand bend then ends near a house.

18. Fork right onto a waymarked path descending through cork woods. The path becomes a rough track and drops to meet a lane. Turn right, following the road downhill and round a left-hand bend. Go round a right-hand bend by a house on the left and continue downhill to a T-junction. Turn left and descend to another T-junction, this time with a wider road. Turn left again, keeping ahead towards Monchique at the next junction. Pass a fruiterer's and reach a roundabout near a large Intermarché supermarket at the bottom end of the town.

19. Turn right at the roundabout, then immediately cross to join a road climbing to the left (there's an information board at the bottom of the street). Emerge in a wide, open square. Directly

ahead is a roundabout and tourist information centre, while to your left is a small supermarket and the Miradouro da Serra.

Highlights

Picota

At 774m, Picota is the second-highest mountain in the Algarve and one of the region's most magnificent viewpoints. The slopes of the mountain are extensively forested and contain important remnants of the Algarve's native woodland, including various species of oak and also chestnut, which grow well in the relatively wet, humid climate. Around 76,000 hectares (760km^2) of land around Monchique – including Picota – form part of the European network of nature protection areas known as Natura 2000.

Monchique

Nestling between wooded mountain slopes, Monchique is a popular destination for hikers and other outdoor enthusiasts. The town itself is also worth exploring, particularly the steep, narrow streets surrounding the town centre. Here you will find a number of shops selling local craft items, many of them made using traditional skills handed down through the generations, and pass numerous examples of traditional Algarvean architecture. Not to be missed either is the Loja do Mel e do Medronho (honey and firewater shop), where it is possible to sample and buy several varieties of locally produced *medronho*, a heady spirit made from the fruits of the strawberry tree.

For photographs visit www.pinterest.co.uk/thewalkerswife

Day 11: Monchique to Marmelete

Once out of Monchique, the Via Algarviana climbs along a winding woodland trail, eventually emerging on a road below the summit of Fóia. The main trail bypasses the high point to the north (a detour can easily be made) then tacks back round the head of a beautiful valley to the west of the summit. It then starts to descend in earnest, leaving the open hills and plunging into a large area of woodland between Fóia and Marmelete. There's one more unexpected climb – near the popular local viewpoint of Picos – followed by a sharp descent to a road and picnic site on the outskirts of Marmelete.

Start: Tourist information centre, Monchique

Finish: At the bottom of Largo Coronel Artur Moreira in Marmelete, not far from the parish church

Distance: 16km

Total ascent: 696m

Total descent: 761m

Time: 4hrs

Terrain: Steep woodland climb to just below the summit of Fóia (902m), then a lovely gentle descent across cultivated mountain slopes. Approaching Marmelete, the trail continues along forestry tracks, mainly downhill but with a short sting in the tail near the small, steep hill of Picos.

Refreshments: There is a snack bar on the summit of Fóia (closed Saturdays), but no other opportunities to purchase refreshments between Monchique and Marmelete. Despite its modest size, there are three restaurants in Marmelete: 'Luz', 'O Tita' and 'Sol da

Serra'. These can be found on the main road running along the top of the village, where there is also a mini-market.

Accommodation: Accommodation is hard to come by in Marmelete, though the Junta de Freguesia (parish council) should be able to arrange for you to spend a night in a municipal dorm in the Casa do Povo – email info@jf-marmelete.pt for details. If planning to follow the alternative coastal route to Cabo de São Vicente, you may prefer to combine two stages and finish the day in Aljezur.

Walking instructions

1. From outside the Miradouro da Serra, cross the roundabout towards the tourist information centre. Go past the building and across the square, then drop left to join the road heading downhill into the centre of Monchique. This emerges in the town's main square. Behind you to the right is Monchique's famous Loja do Mel e do Medronho (honey and firewater shop).

2. Cross towards the far left-hand corner of the square. Climb for a short distance along a cobbled street with steps down the middle, then take a narrow alleyway on the left – the Travessa das Guerreiras. Climb steeply between buildings.

3. At the top of the alley, keep ahead across a cobbled street on to a narrow, cobbled road opposite. Go round a right-hand bend, then turn immediately left into Rua Costa Goodolfim. Keep to the right of the yellow house ahead (number 9). With three terraced houses ahead (numbers 9, 8 and 7), take the track turning sharply right towards a Via Algarviana signpost. Bear left, then continue to ascend diagonally across the slope. At the top of the main cobbled street, keep ahead on to a smaller, rougher track. This turns sharply left, ending at the Convento de Nossa Senhora De Desterro (an old ruined convent – see below).

4. Take a path to the right just before the building. Fork left immediately above the old convent and climb through woods. Join a stony path and bear left alongside a wall until you emerge on a two-lane road. Turn left, now climbing more gently. After about 50 metres, turn sharply right to continue on a woodland path. At a junction, turn left on to a narrower path and climb steadily, eventually emerging on the corner of a wider gravel track.

5. Keep ahead up the hill. At a fork (there are houses below to the left), keep right along the upper, main track. Climb to the right, then go round a sharp right-hand bend. The track turns back to the left and levels off. Continue uphill on to open hillside, passing a grassy track on the left signed as part of a local 'PR' route. As the main gravel track curves left in front of eucalyptus trees, fork right on to a rougher, stony track.

6. At the top of the climb, join a road and continue ahead towards the various masts and buildings on the summit of Fóia. After about 700 metres, the Via Algarviana forks right on to a path running below the level of the road. (You can visit the summit quite easily by continuing along the road – retrace your steps to rejoin the Via Algarviana or follow the signed PR route down the north side of the mountain.)

7. On meeting a fence, go through an awkward swing gate and continue on to a grassy path. Follow this down to meet an overgrown gravel track just before a small reservoir. Turn left for a short distance, then take a path on the right. Pass to the left of the reservoir and reach another awkward swing gate leading on to a road. Cross straight over and on to a gravel track. Descend gently, entering eucalyptus woods. Emerge back into the open and shortly reach a junction of tracks just above an abandoned house.

8. Turn sharply left, following a Via Algarviana sign. The track curves round the head of a valley, crossing a small stream, then continues past a number of abandoned agricultural terraces. At a

fork, continue along the level track bearing right. A short distance ahead, keep ahead on to a smaller, level track signed to Marmelete. After a sharp left-hand bend, the track climbs to a junction with a wider gravel track.

9. Turn sharp right and follow the track downhill along a line of wind turbines. Where indicated, turn left on to a smaller track leading into woodland. This quickly reaches a fork; take the lower, right-hand track. Leaving the trees, bear steeply downhill to the right and join another track bearing left. The track winds downhill then climbs briefly through pine woods. Descend again, then fork right to drop to a road.

10. Cross straight over the road and continue downhill along a forest track. On reaching a fork, bear right so as to pass to the left of a meadow in a valley. The track then starts to climb. Keep straight up the hill, reaching a junction just as the track levels off. Bear right to continue along the main track, which climbs again and ends at a junction with a minor road. If you have the energy, turn left for a final steep climb to the summit of Picos – a popular local viewpoint overlooking Marmelete.

11. The main route follows the road to the right, passing round a left-hand bend and descending through eucalyptus woods. Turn right at a junction with a wider road, passing round another left-hand bend. At a fork, take the track branching left and emerge from woodland near an agricultural building. Continue ahead in the direction of Marmelete, descending steeply on a rough, stony track. After being joined by a track from the right, you will reach a signpost. Continue downhill to a junction with a two-lane road on the outskirts of Marmelete. Just across the road to the left are some shaded picnic tables ('Parque de Merendas').

12. Turn right, towards the centre of Marmelete. Just past signs marking the edge of the village, bear left on to a cobbled road, which follows a route below and roughly parallel to the main road.

Emerge on a tarmac road by a number of information boards, where the section ends. Two snack bars/restaurant – 'Luz' and 'O Tita' – can be found up on the main road to the right. For the Junta da Freguesia/Casa do Povo, keep straight ahead along a continuation of the wide cobbled road (see next section for details).

Highlights

Convento de Nossa Senhora De Desterro

This former Franciscan monastery was founded in 1631 by Pero da Silva, who would later go on to become the viceroy of Portugal's East Indian possessions. The building was badly damaged by the 1755 earthquake and is now largely a ruin, but it retains an air of charm and dilapidated grandeur. The old monastery garden offers a splendid view over Monchique and the surrounding hills, and also contains an imposing magnolia tree (now in a poor state of health) widely believed to have been brought back from India by da Silva himself.

Fóia

With an elevation of 902m, Fóia is the highest mountain in the Algarve region of Portugal. A paved road leads to the very top of the mountain, where there are several buildings, including a chapel, a large snack bar, and a number of telecommunication facilities. Despite this urban sprawl, there's plenty of room to appreciate the view, which on a fine day stretches all the way to the Atlantic Ocean. Below the summit, the Via Algarviana winds gently down through a scenic landscape of mountain pasture and abandoned agricultural terraces, where cattle and other livestock are likely to be encountered grazing freely.

For photographs visit www.pinterest.co.uk/thewalkerswife

Day 12: Marmelete to Barão de São João

Shortly after leaving Marmelete, the Via Algarviana bears left and begins a long descent to the hamlet of Malhão. The trail then continues down the Vagarosa valley to the Odiáxere reservoir, following a quiet two-lane road for a large part of the way. After climbing away from the reservoir, there is a long, gentle descent into the beautiful Sobrosa valley, where the trail crosses and recrosses the river on several occasions. The official end for this section is in Bensafrim, where the valley opens out, but because of a lack of accommodation it is recommended that you continue along the Via Algarviana for a further 6km or so to Barão de São João.

Start: At the bottom of Largo Coronel Artur Moreira in Marmelete, not far from the parish church

Finish: Barão de São João, close to the Casa do Joao

Distance: 37km

Total ascent: 510m

Total descent: 448m

Time: 8hrs

Terrain: Although this is a very long section, the trail is mainly routed along roads or good-quality tracks. There is a long descent from Marmelete then plenty of level walking, though climbs are also encountered near the Odiáxere reservoir and just after leaving Bensafrim. After heavy rain, fords across the Vagarosa and Sobrosa rivers may only be passable by wading.

Refreshments: Along the way, there are cafes in Romeiras and also the Restaurante Solar do Pincho in Pincho (meals are only available here if booked in advance). There are bars, restaurants and a supermarket in Bensafrim and a similar range of choice in Barão de São Jão.

Accommodation: There's nothing really suitable for walkers in Bensafrim, so it's recommended that you extend the section to Barão de São Jão, where you can find en-suite accommodation in the Casa do Joao.

Walking instructions

1. From the information boards in Marmelete, continue ahead along the wide cobbled road signed to the Junta da Freguesia. This descends gently, curving left and passing a water tap. Where the road opens out, bear slightly right, then turn left, following another sign for the Junta da Freguesia. (For the Casa do Povo, keep ahead to a T-junction, then turn right and right again, on to the Rua da Escola. Follow this street up to the main road at the top of the village.)

2. The road drops to a right-hand bend then continues on a level along the bottom edge of the village. Pass public toilets and the Junta da Freguesia (where free internet access is available and you can pick up keys for the Casa do Povo) and follow the cobbled road round a left-hand bend. Climb past a picnic bench and viewpoint, joining a tarmac road. Continue uphill to the main two-lane road through the village and turn left.

3. After just under a kilometre along the main road, turn left on to a track marked by a Via Algarviana sign for Bensafrim (this is about 100 metres after the link route to Aljezur forks off to the right). The track meanders along the top edge of a wooded valley. Ignore a left fork descending into the valley and continue along the main track, which follows the crest of a ridge. At a clear fork, take the lower, right-hand track heading away from the valley and back into woodland. The track soon returns to the ridge but then curves right

and descends through eucalyptus woods. After a brief climb, descend again to a junction of tracks in a dip.

4. Turn sharply left to continue downhill. The track descends into a valley, passing through the hamlet of Malhão. Follow the valley down to a junction with another gravel track and turn right. Continue down the valley, the land rising steeply to your left and a small stream below on the right. Ignore a signed track on the right to Zebro and Azenha, and continue ahead. Where the valley opens up by a small lake, reach a junction with a two-lane road.

5. Turn left, following a Via Algarviana sign for Bensafrim. The road passes through the scattered community of Romeiras, passing a cafe on the left and another on the right. Climb gently out of the hamlet and continue ahead until the road starts to climb to the right (this is about 2.5km after joining the road and at a point where two distant wind turbines are clearly visible ahead). Fork left on to a track (there's a Via Algarviana sign) and continue down the valley to a reservoir. Keep the reservoir to your left and then cut right, following another arm of the reservoir away from the main lake. Cross a stream and climb back up to the main road left earlier.

6. Turn left and follow the road back towards the reservoir. As you approach the first inlet, turn right up a smaller road towards some ruined farm buildings. Bear left past the ruins, then drop right to return to the main road. Turn right and follow the main road round a sharp left-hand bend signed to Lagos. Climb gently until a waymarked track appears on your right. Join this and climb above and parallel to the road through eucalyptus trees. The trees open out near the top of the hill, revealing excellent panoramic views. Drop back down to the road and turn right, shortly passing a sign indicating that you have crossed into the municipality of Lagos.

7. Follow the road round a right-hand bend. Just before a bridge over a stream, fork right on to a gravel track signed to Vale do

Lobo and begin a long, gentle climb. The track bears slightly left below a house, shortly passing a second dwelling. Ignore the next track forking right, instead keeping to the main track, which bears left. After a sharp left-hand bend, climb out of the valley and up to a cross track on the brow of the hill. Keep straight ahead, passing to the right of a small lake, and follow the track gently downhill until a junction with a two-lane road is reached.

8. Follow the road to the right, reaching a right-hand bend after about 250 metres. Continue ahead down a track signed to Bensafrim. (Refreshments can be found a further 200 metres up the road to the right at the Restaurante Solar do Pincho.) The track follows a level route along a valley bottom, crossing and recrossing a small stream. At a fork, stick to the main track on the left – that is, the one furthest from the stream. Returning to the stream, the track crosses to the right bank, after which the valley begins to open out, eucalyptus trees appearing to your right. When you see the river next it is noticeably larger, having been joined by another.

9. After passing a ford and track on the left, the track bears right, away from the river, towards electricity wires. Continue across a wide, open valley, eventually regaining contact with the river where the valley narrows. As you approach Bensafrim, join a tarmac lane and follow it to a fork. Bear right, following a road sign for Fronteira. As you approach the town proper, pass an old wash house and cross a bridge over a stream on to a cobbled street.

10. The official route follows the street forking right – the Rua da Igreja. However, if you want to avoid a convoluted tour of Bensafrim, you may prefer to fork left along Rua do Rossio. If you do, turn left immediately after house number 15 on to a narrow street (Travessa Julio Dantas) to emerge on the corner of the main road out of Bensafrim.

11. Following the official route, continue up to a junction of narrow streets. Keep ahead for a few metres, then bear left on to Rua dos

Peitoris. At the end of the street, fork right and then turn immediately left. Pass the apricot-coloured Vicentina building, then keep ahead through a narrow passageway and back out on to another street. At a junction with a larger road, continue ahead until you reach an information board to the rear of the Pastelaria snack bar.

12. To leave Bensafrim, walk towards the front of the bar. From here, turn left to meet the corner of a cobbled street. Keep ahead past a pharmacy. At the end of the road, turn right and then immediately left, passing the 'O Koala' restaurant. Follow the road down to a junction opposite a *supermercado*. Turn right and then immediately left, down the side of the shop. Take the next narrow street on the right, Travessa Julio Dantas, where you are joined by the more direct alternative route described above. Shortly emerge on the corner of the main road out of Bensafrim.

13. Keep ahead to cross a narrow road bridge with care. Immediately after the bridge, turn right on to a smaller road, following a Via Algarviana sign. Ignore the next road forking uphill to the left (this is signed as the link route to Lagos) and continue ahead until you reach another road forking left not far before a motorway flyover. Take this road, which passes below the flyover and then climbs steeply. At a left-hand bend, fork right on to a gravel track.

14. At a three-way fork, keep ahead along the main track. Keep ahead again at the next fork, ignoring a track forking left to a house. Once past the house, follow the track sharply right, alongside a fence. The main gravel track shortly curves right, in the direction of a house, but keep ahead on to a smaller, grassier track which continues to follow the fence. At the next junction, take the track turning sharply left, past a ruined house, and follow a lovely winding route through a cork forest. On reaching a wider sandier track, bear left.

15. With a fence and open field ahead, bear right. The track follows a fence to a fork. Keep ahead towards a house, passing to the left of the building. Follow the track ahead until you reach a junction with a road and turn right.

16. At a group of houses, turn left on to a smaller lane. Entirely concealed to the right of the lane is the Zoo de Lagos (Lagos Zoo) (the entrance is at the opposite end of the grounds). Follow the lane to a junction with houses ahead and turn right. The road drops to a T-junction with a two-lane road.

17. Turn left, towards the village of Barão de São Jão. Walk past the church and keep ahead along the main cobbled street. With Café Central ahead, follow a cobbled street to the right. The section ends just outside the mini-market below the Casa do Joao. You can ask about accommodation in the shop or follow the road round to the entrance off Rua das Parreiras (see start of next section for route details).

Highlight

Albufeira de Odiáxere

The jagged shoreline of the Albufeira de Odiáxere (the Odiáxere reservoir) was formed in the late 1950s/early 1960s, when a dam was built across the Odiáxere river to create a reliable water supply for the growing towns and resorts on the coast. The reservoir's wooded basin is now a popular recreational area, attracting weekend picnickers as well as hikers, particularly near the dam at the southern end of the lake.

For photographs visit www.pinterest.co.uk/thewalkerswife

Day 13: Barão de São Jão to Vila do Bispo

From Barão de São Jão, the Via Algarviana climbs into a large stone pine forest – part of a designated protected area known as the Perimetro Florestal do Barão de São João (Barão de São João Forest Perimeter). Undulating tracks pass through a mix of forest and more open areas – including past an important wetland habitat, the Lagoa de Budens – before descending back towards the coast near Raposeira. The final few kilometres provide a foretaste of the final day's walk through the wide, open fields and coastal scrub of the Costa Vicentina.

Start: Barão de São Jão, close to the Casa do Joao
Finish: The Praça da República, in the centre of Vila do Bispo near the main church
Distance: 24km
Total ascent: 470m
Total descent: 448m
Time: 7hrs
Terrain: For most of the section, the trail follows undulating but good-quality tracks – initially through stone pine forest but later through an open, agricultural landscape.
Refreshments: The Casa do Pasto is a restaurant and bar just off the main route in Raposeira. Vila do Bispo contains a wide selection of bars, shops and restaurants, including a Lidl supermarket.
Accommodation: The Casa Mestre, the Hotel Mira Sagres and the Pure Flor de Esteva (bed and breakfast) are all located close to the

centre of Vila do Bispo, while a five-minute walk from the town is the Quinta da Pedra. Accommodation is also available at the Good Feeling Hostel in Raposeira.

Walking instructions

1. Follow the road up the hill from the mini-market below the Casa do Joao. Fork to the right of a sandy-coloured building, then take the next street on the right, towards the Atabai Bar. Turn right for a few metres and then left on to Rua da Bica. (The road to the right is the Rua das Parreiras, which will take you down to the Casa do Joao's guest entrance.) Descend gently past cultivated plots to reach a fork in a dip. Take the cobbled road climbing to the right.

2. Approaching the top of the rise, turn left on to a track signed to Vila do Bispo. Climb steadily through woodland on a stony track. Eventually emerge at a junction with a wider stony track with open views ahead and wind turbines to your left. Turn left, now gently ascending. Just before the turbines, note a beacon on the right marking the summit of the hill. The track bears left to a cross junction of forestry tracks.

3. Keep ahead on to a track signed to Vinha Velha. At a fork, bear right, again signed to Vinha Velha. The track descends, emerging from trees into a grassy open area (there are wind turbines visible on the skyline ahead, and in the distance can be seen the golf resort of Parque de Floresta). Keep ahead past the complex of buildings comprising Vinha Velha, a small community practising permaculture.

4. At the next fork, bear right on to a smaller track running below pine trees with a field to the right. Pass a track forking left; a short distance ahead, fork right by a pond. The track climbs gently then drops to cross a muddy pool (fordable). Climb towards wind turbines, following the main track as it curves left and then right. There's a very steep climb, then the track levels off. Climb more

easily to the top of the hill, wind turbines ahead. At a junction, bear right and follow a track curving left through woodland towards turbines. At a junction with a wider track, turn left and immediately reach a junction with a wide forest road.

5. Bear left. Stick to the main track, which curves right where a smaller gravel track keeps straight ahead. The track climbs again, then curves left along the crest of the ridge, passing directly below a wind turbine. At an obvious fork in the main track, bear right. Climb gently then continue along an undulating track through stone pine forest. At an obvious fork, take the lower, left-hand track. The forest opens out into scrubland, the track passing a ruined farm building.

6. Just beyond the farm ruin, bear right at a junction. The track curves left, passing a house tucked away in a dip to the right. Pass a track on the right, a beacon visible a few metres along it. Continue along the main track, passing another ruin, and eventually curve right into more pine woodland. Ignore any lesser tracks to the left or right, and continue until you reach a major cross track by a stand of pine.

7. Keep straight ahead, in the direction of wind turbines, passing a track on the right signed to Vale da Ra. Continue along a long, straight track, eventually emerging on a wide, open plain with wetland to the left and wind turbines ahead. As you approach woodland again, bear right at a cross junction of tracks into the trees. The track soon re-emerges from the woods, crossing a wide grassy area on which several wind turbines are sited. Keep ahead along the main track, which passes to the left of solar panels and enters an area of eucalyptus trees. Leaving these, approach more wind turbines and take the track forking left just in front of them. At a sandy junction, stick to the main track, which curves left and drops to a major two-lane road. (In May 2015, it looked like a new

road was being constructed along the line of the track, so details of the route described above are likely to have altered.)

8. Follow the main road to the right for a short distance, then cross carefully to a track on the other side. Turn left, climbing gently above the road. After about 200 metres, the track curves right, climbing away from the road. Crest the brow of a hill and continue along a pleasant level track with great views down towards the coast. The track drops into a valley, curving right. After a left-hand bend, turn right at a signpost, crossing a stream and continuing straight up a lane ahead. Climb steeply before the road levels off.

9. Vila do Bispo comes into view as you crest the brow of a hill. Follow the lane sharply to the left and continue to a junction with a wider road. Turn right, heading down the hill towards the village of Raposeira. At the bottom of the hill, keep ahead past roads to the left and right. Take the next road on the left, indicated by a Via Algarviana sign. Alternatively, you may wish to continue round a right-hand bend to the Casa do Pasto, a restaurant and bar in Raposeira.

10. Where the tarmac ends ahead, fork right on to a lane. This climbs steadily to the left (away from Vila do Bispo). Just before the tarmac ends (the sea is visible ahead), take a track on the right heading back towards Vila do Bispo. Drop into a valley then climb gently up towards the town. Turn left at a tarmac road, up to a T-junction, and then right, over a bridge across a main road and into Vila do Bispo. Keep ahead across a two-lane road (there's a zebra crossing to the right) and follow a road past the church and into the centre of town. The section finishes by an information board for the Rota Vicentina (the GR11) opposite the Casa Mestre in the main square.

Highlight

Perimetro Florestal do Barão de São João (Barão de São João Forest Perimeter)

The Barão de São João Forest is a protected stone pine forest – part of the Natura 2000 network of European nature reserves – covering more than 200 hectares. As well as being an important habitat for wildlife, the forest is also a popular recreational area. Waymarked trails attract hikers, runners and mountain bikers, while picnic tables dotted around the woods provide a number of cool, shady spots in which to enjoy a picnic.

For photographs visit www.pinterest.co.uk/thewalkerswife

Day 14: Vila do Bispo to Cabo de São Vicente

There are two waymarked routes to Cabo de São Vicente from Vila do Bispo: the Via Algarviana (GR13) and the Rota Vicentina (GR11). The Via Algarviana heads south, across a relatively flat coastal plain, only emerging on the coast for the final few kilometres of the stage. The region's wide open landscapes – comprised of low-lying scrub, rough grazing and arable fields – are very different from anything previously encountered on the trail. After reaching Portugal's southern coast, the trail joins the Ecovia do Litoral, a long-distance bike path, for a dramatic coastal approach to the lighthouse and cape.

Start: The Praça da República, in the centre of Vila do Bispo near the main church

Finish: Cabo de São Vicente

Distance: 17km

Total ascent: 160m

Total descent: 211m

Time: 5hrs

Terrain: For most of the section, the trail follows good-quality tracks and minor roads across a flat coastal plain. Approaching Cabo de São Vicente, the trail joins a cycle track alongside a busy road before veering away from the road to join a rugged coastal path.

Refreshments: A range of snacks and drinks can be bought from stalls outside the fortress at Cabo de São Vicente – though be prepared to pay a premium. There's also a cafe bar inside the fortress.

Accommodation: The nearest accommodation to the end of the trail can be found in Sagres, a short bus journey or 6km walk along the Ecovia do Litoral (see 'Accessing the Via Algarviana' in the Introduction). There's plenty of choice here, but you can also continue on the bus back to Vila do Bispo or on to Lagos – a beautiful city with numerous places to stay.

Walking instructions

1. From the main square in Vila do Bispo, ignore a GR11 sign for 'Cabo de S. Vicente' (unless you wish to join the alternative coastal route for the final stage of your journey); instead retrace the previous day's route back past the church and across the bridge over the main road. Stick with the road as it curves round to the right and back towards the main road. About 50 metres before a junction, fork left on to a lane running parallel to the road.

2. At a fork, bear left, away from the main road. Follow the lane to its end, then bear right to continue on a gravel track. As you approach a low rise, leave the main track, which bears right, and continue ahead on a smaller track over the rise. As you crest the top of the hill, you will be able to see the town of Sagres directly ahead. Continue ahead until you reach a junction with another track, close to a fence on your left.

3. Turn right, so that you are heading roughly north-west. The track eventually meets a minor road directly below the main road between Sagres and Vila do Bispo. Keep ahead through the underpass, then turn immediately left on to a lane running parallel to the main road.

4. At a T-junction, turn right, away from the main road, towards a group of farm buildings. Joining a wide gravel track, swing left past the buildings (Herdade dos Covões) and then uphill to the

right. Climb gently to another large farm complex and continue to a fork in the track, a short distance before a junction with a road.

5. Take the left fork and turn left again along the road. Where the surfaced road ends, keep ahead along a gravel track. Just ahead is a stand of scrubby pine wood. Before reaching the trees, follow the main track round a sharp right-hand bend and continue to a T-junction with another track.

6. Turn left and join the signed route of the GR11 path ('Cabo de S. Vicente'). Follow the wide gravel track towards an abandoned village (Vale Santo), the lighthouse on the cape coming into view for the first time. The track curves left through the village then turns into a surfaced lane. Follow the long, straight road across the coastal plain to a T-junction with a busy two-lane road.

7. Cross carefully and turn right along a gravel strip for the use of cyclists and pedestrians. Pass a restaurant/handicraft centre on the right and a former coastal fort, Forte do Beliche, on the left. Where indicated, cross the road to the right and follow a rough, sandy track away from the road until you emerge on cliffs above a spectacular crescent-shaped bay.

8. Turn left, back towards the prominent lighthouse at Cabo de São Vicente. Follow a rough, stony track, initially in the direction of the lighthouse, then more to the left, so that you re-emerge on the road. Turn right and pass through a large parking area full of food and souvenir stalls. Strangely, there is nothing to mark the end of the Via Algarviana, although there is a board to mark the end of the Rota Vicentina. Inside the fort (closed on Mondays) is a supersized chair with the lighthouse behind – a much better spot for an end of walk photograph.

Highlights

Forte do Beliche

The Beliche fort was built some time during the 16th century to control shipping along the coast and to protect Portuguese fishermen from attack by pirates. At the entrance to the fort can be seen the royal coat of arms of King Philip IV of Spain (Philip or Felipe III in Portugal) and an inscription dated 1632, indicating the completion of major reconstruction work in this year. The earthquake of 1755 caused severe damage to the fort's structure, and in the decades that followed it was gradually abandoned. The outer walls were restored and made safe in 1960, at which time a teahouse was built over the foundations of the former barracks.

Cabo de São Vicente

Europe's most south-westerly point, Cabo de São Vicente (or Cape St Vincent as it is better known in English) has been regarded as a sacred spot for millennia: the place where the world ended and the sun sank into the ocean. (The cape's spectacular sunsets still draw large crowds of spectators.) In later years, the cape became an important landmark for ships heading for the Mediterranean, and the site of numerous naval battles. A fort was first built on the cape in the 16th century in an attempt to control shipping and protect nearby coastal settlements from raiders (it was rebuilt twice in the 17th and 18th centuries). A primitive lighthouse was also constructed – a crude warning beacon cared for by a group of Franciscan friars living on the cape. This was replaced by the present lighthouse – one of the most powerful in Europe – in 1846.

For photographs visit www.pinterest.co.uk/thewalkerswife

Alternative finish via Aljezur and the Rota Vicentina (GR11)

The alternative finish to Cabo de São Vicente follows a section of undulating clifftop path known as the Trilho dos Pescadores or Fishermen's Trail. This is marked using similar principles but in green and blue.

Allow an additional three days for this route.

Day 12: Marmelete to Aljezur

After splitting from the main trail west of Marmelete, the link route to Aljezur descends steeply through a eucalyptus plantation into the narrow Ribeira da Cerca valley. A shaded track continues down the valley as far as Moinho do Bispo ('bishop's mill'), crossing the stream on a number of occasions. The trail then becomes more difficult, following an undulating route across wooded ridges and over the Corvo viewpoint. Entering Aljezur, it passes close to the main church before crossing the valley to the municipal market below Aljezur Castle.

Start: Marmelete

Finish: Aljezur Market

Distance: 19km

Total ascent: 364m

Total descent: 742m

Time: 5hrs

Terrain: Some road walking near the start and finish of the section, but mostly good-quality gravel tracks. These head mainly downhill to begin with, but the second half of the section is far more undulating.

Refreshments: Refreshments are only available at the start and finish of the section. Aljezur contains a number of cafe bars and restaurants, a municipal marketplace, and a large Intermarché supermarket.

Accommodation: There are three main places to stay in Aljezur: A Lareira (a restaurant with rooms), the Vicentina Hotel, and the Amazigh Design Hostel.

Walking instructions

1. Leave Marmelete following instructions for Day 12 of the main route between Marmelete and Barão de São Jão. After a little under a kilometre along the main road – and about 100 metres before the main route turns off to the left – look out for a Via Algarviana sign on the right ('Aljezur 16.7km'). Join a track winding downhill into a valley. At a dip where the track rises ahead, take a track turning sharply right signed to Rocha and Aljezur. This continues down into the valley, shortly bending left.

2. At the bottom of the hill, cross a stream and continue along the right-hand side of the valley. The track passes some houses and abandoned farms. Just past one abandoned barn, follow the track to the right, up into a side valley, then turn sharp left at a fork to return to the main valley. The track then dips to cross the stream again and continues down the left-hand side of the valley.

3. Reach a junction with a better stone track and turn left to continue down the valley. At a fork, keep left along the main level track, which eventually returns to the stream. If water levels are high, use a concrete bridge to the left to cross and continue ahead down the valley. Shortly after passing above a group of houses to the left (Moinho do Bispo), the track turns sharp right. On a sharp left-hand bend soon after, take a waymarked smaller track heading uphill to the right.

4. The track climbs through thick eucalyptus and round a hairpin bend to the left. Emerge into a more open area and fork right to continue climbing. As the track bears left, the gradient lessens. Pass through further stands of eucalyptus and continue climbing until you reach a more open area where you are joined by a track from the left. A short distance ahead, at a junction below electricity wires, bear left.

5. At the crest of the hill, with fine views ahead, fork left past eucalyptus trees. A yellow marker below the white and red waymark indicates the presence of a local PR route. At the next fork, a short distance ahead, bear right. Continue along an undulating track with views opening out towards the coast. After passing a track on the right, you will reach a fork. Take the lower, left-hand track descending into eucalyptus woods. The descent is followed by a short, steep climb back up to a wooded ridge. There is another sharp incline before the track reaches an unexpected house at the top of the hill.

6. Drop left into a dip, then climb quite steeply to the right. At a track junction at the top, bear right again, views opening out towards the sea as the track continues to gain height. Follow the track to the left, through a mix of pine and eucalyptus trees, then reach a junction where the main track turns downhill to the right. Keep straight ahead and climb steeply through eucalyptus woods.

7. At the top of the hill, bear right along the crest of a ridge. Descend to a fork in a dip, where you should be able to see beehives to your left. Take the track bearing right. Climb to the right of a hill, then bear left where signed for Aljezur. A steep climb leads to a trig point on the summit of Corvo.

8. From the hilltop, the track curves right, along the line of the ridge, and then to the left. Aljezur is now clearly visible ahead. Climb again then bear slightly right, descending towards a red-brick wall with kennels and dogs to the left. Bear left along an undulating track. After passing two stone ruins, reach a junction in front of a fence and water tanks. Turn right, passing in front of the tanks, then descend to where another track crosses the line of your route. Take the track to the left and descend to a junction with a road on the edge of Aljezur.

9. Take the smaller road ahead to the left of houses, then continue on to a track descending along the edge of pine woods. At the

bottom of the hill, turn right at a road and climb back up into the town. Turn left at the top of the hill in front of a public shelter and head towards a large mustard-coloured building at the back of an open square used for parking. Join a cobbled street to the right of the building and emerge in a square in front of the parish church. The square is a popular local meeting point and contains a couple of cafe bars.

10. Keep ahead, passing to the left of the church, and join a road continuing down the hill – a red-and-white cross indicating that this is not the correct route appears to have been placed on this road by mistake. Follow the road down to a roundabout, where the Hotel Vicentina (adjacent to a large supermarket) can be found to the right. The main route continues ahead, towards the older part of Aljezur on the opposite side of the valley. The section ends in the car park for the municipal market on the right, a short distance from restaurants and the Amazigh Design Hostel.

Highlight

Igreja Nova

The town of Aljezur consists of two distinct settlements divided by a wide level valley. The newer of these settlements, Igreja Nova ('new church'), is the part you will encounter first when walking from Marmelete and was built following the devastating earthquake of 1755 as a means of persuading local people to remain in Aljezur. Less constrained by the geography of the valley, Igreja Nova is now the main area of expansion in the town and the location for most of its civic facilities.

For photographs visit www.pinterest.co.uk/thewalkerswife

Day 13: Aljezur to Arrifana

This is a short day's walk, though one that can easily be extended either by continuing along the Historical Way towards Bordeira and Carrapateira (see next section) or by incorporating the coastal Ponta da Atalaia Circuit (an extra 6km) into your walk (for details visit en.rotavicentina.com). The main route described below passes through an attractive and varied landscape, with bands of pine and eucalyptus trees interspersed with more open, agricultural areas. Glimpses of the sea become more frequent towards Arrifana, with tantalizing views of the rugged Atlantic coast to the south.

Start: Aljezur Market
Finish: Arrifana
Distance: 12km
Total ascent: 224m
Total descent: 184m
Time: 4hrs
Terrain: Mainly good-quality gravel tracks, with some shorter sections of potentially busy road walking. Much flatter than many sections of the Via Algarviana though still quite undulating.
Refreshments: There are plenty of bars and restaurants in Arrifana. The nearest supermarket, however, is some 2km off the main route in Vale de Telha. To find it, follow the signed road down into the estate and then ahead across two roundabouts.
Accommodation: There are plenty of places to stay in Arrifana, including the Arrifana Retreat, the Arrifana Lounge Guest House and an attractive youth hostel. Lodging rooms are also available

above the Restaurante Oceano. There are more possible places to stay in nearby Vale da Telha, including the Hotel Vale da Telha and the Ocean Life Guest House.

Walking instructions

1. From the municipal market in Aljezur, follow GR11 (E9) signs for Odeiceixe and Arrifana across a metal footbridge over the Aljezur river. This replaced a triple-arched medieval bridge washed away during floods in March 1947 and leads into the town's historic centre. Turn right on to a cobbled street – Rua João Dias Mendes – in front of the Amazigh Hostel. Climb along a cobbled street to a fork, then bear left, following signs for the castle, church and museum. After passing the municipal museum, the GR11 splits. Follow the sign for Arrifana to the left and head steeply uphill towards Igreja de Misericórdia ('the church of mercy'). This 16th-century building was Aljezur's parish church until 1809, when the centre of the parish was moved to Igreja Nova.

2. From the church, you have the choice of forking left and tackling a final steep climb to Aljezur's castle (recommended) or of continuing along the GR11 by forking to the right of the church and then bearing left on to a concrete track descending into a valley. Continue along the bottom of the valley until you start to wind your way up through a new development. Ignore a fork on the right and begin a long, steep, winding climb. As you ascend, the Atlantic Ocean becomes visible to the west. Reach a fork at the top of the climb and take the track to the right, through stone pine trees. Descend gently to a two-lane road and turn right.

3. Follow a level road through pine forest for around 400 metres. Just before a concrete hut, turn left on to a track signed to Arrifana. A winding descent leads down into a valley through pine woods. Near the bottom of the hill, bear right. Where a steep track climbs

straight ahead, take a track bearing left into eucalyptus woods. A long, steady climb, steep in places, leads back out of the valley. After the track levels off, keep ahead, ignoring a track to the right. Climb gently and reach a T-junction of tracks, with Arrifana signed in both directions: 14km to the right and 8km to the left. The route to the right is part of the Ponta da Atalaia Circuit and provides an alternative coastal approach to Arrifana.

4. To continue along the GR11 (the Historical Way), turn left and follow the track for around 600 metres as far as a stone ruin on the left. This is just past a stand of eucalyptus trees and adjacent to a junction of tracks. Take the track descending gently to the right then climb gently to a junction with a two-way road. A track to the right is signed to the Quinta Do Largo Silencioso (accommodation). Follow the road to the left, watching out for fast-moving traffic.

5. After about 250 metres, bear right on to a concrete track signed to Arrifana. Just past a small group of houses on the right, the track turns sharply left and then sharply right in front of a ruined farm. At a cross track with a villa to the right, keep ahead on to a gravel track. The track winds through eucalyptus trees before emerging in a more open area. Drop gently to the right of a ruined farmhouse. As you climb out of the dip, Arrifana Bay becomes visible to the right.

6. Continue to a track junction on the crest of the next rise and turn right. Ignore a smaller track continuing ahead and stick to the main track bearing left. Views now open up along the wild rugged coast to the south. Bear right where indicated to reach a signed junction: Carrapateira 21.7km to the left and Arrifana 2.5km to the right. If continuing towards Carrapateira, turn left, otherwise bear right and drop to a junction with a two-lane road.

7. Turn left up the hill towards Arrifana. After the first few houses, pass a road on the right signed to Vale de Telha. (For the Arrifana Retreat, turn right here then follow the next street on the right to its

end.) Continuing into Arrifana, follow the main road round a right-hand bend and then downhill past the youth hostel. On a left-hand bend, your route meets up with the Fishermen's Trail, which rejoins the main GR11 from the right. Continue down the road to where a concrete track on the left descends to the beach. You can finish your walk here or continue to the fortress and viewpoint on the headland overlooking the bay.

Highlights

Aljezur Castle

Aljezur Castle is one of seven former Moorish fortifications reputedly represented on the Portuguese national flag. Now a ruin, its walls still provide splendid panoramic views, including along the Aljezur river towards the coast. From here it is easy to imagine what the river must have looked like several centuries ago, before silting up. At that time, Aljezur was a bustling river port and the castle served an important function in defending the town from attacks by Barbary pirates.

The Rota Vicentina

The Rota Vicentina comprises a network of walking trails along Portugal's south-west coast. The main long-distance trail is the Historical Way or GR11, which stretches for some 230km between Santiago do Cacém and Cabo de São Vicente, mainly along historical tracks and pathways. Complementing the GR route is the Fishermen's Trail, a more demanding path hugging the wild Atlantic coastline as closely as possible. This latter trail consists of four linear sections (between Porto Covo and Odeceixe) and five complementary coastal circuits. The last of these – the Telheiro Beach Circuit – forms part of the alternative finish to the Via Algarviana.

For photographs visit www.pinterest.co.uk/thewalkerswife

Day 14: Arrifana to Carrapateira

Between Arrifana and Carrapateira the Historical Way follows a mainly inland route, out of sight of the nearby Atlantic Ocean. However, the walk does offer one memorable coastal view: from the cliffs above Praia do Canal a short distance to the south of Arrifana. Beyond Canal, the trail crosses an undulating landscape of mixed woodland and farmland before following an attractive valley down to the picture-postcard village of Bordeira. Carrapateira is now under 6km away – but on the other side of a steep wooded hill. More sea views from the top are followed by a gentle descent to Carrapateira.

Start: Arrifana
Finish: Carrapateira
Distance: 24km
Total ascent: 413m
Total descent: 500m
Time: 7hrs
Terrain: For most of the section, the trail is routed along good-quality gravel tracks. However, care should be taken on the steep, stony descent to Praia do Canal.
Refreshments: There is a cafe in Bordeira (closed Mondays) and also a water tap. The Restaurante do Cabrita and Restaurante L-Colesterol are on the outskirts of Carrapateira, while in the centre of the village you will find a mini mercado and a number of bars serving snack-type meals, including a vegan cafe.
Accommodation: The Casa da Estela, Carrapateira Lodge and Pensão das Dunas offer bed and breakfast accommodation in or

around the centre of Carrapateira, while just to the north of the village are the luxurious Casa Fajara hotel and the L-Colesterol Bed & Breakfast. More accommodation can be found at Monte do Sapeiro and Monte da Vilarinha, a few kilometres into the next day's section near the village of Vilarinha.

Walking instructions

1. Retrace your steps up the road leading out of Arrifana until you reach a track on the right signed to Aljezur and Carrapateira. Still retracing your steps from yesterday (assuming you followed the Historical Way into Arrifana), follow the track up the hill. You will pass a track on the left then shortly reach a signpost where the trail from Arrifana divides into northbound and southbound routes. Continue ahead, past the track on the left, following a sign for Carrapateira.

2. At a fork, take the lower, left-hand track and descend through stone pine forest. Soon after the track starts to climb, you will reach another clear fork. Bear right. As you crest the brow of a hill, a long sweep of rugged coastline appears ahead, stretching southwards into the distance. Descend towards the bay at Canal, eventually bearing left and continuing downhill on a rough, steep track to the valley floor.

3. Bear right towards the beach and then turn left on to a track running behind it. This becomes a clear, winding track climbing out of the valley. Once on to the cliffs, the track heads inland, now climbing more gently through a mix of pine and eucalyptus trees. After a slight right-hand bend, you will reach a long, straight, level section, initially through eucalyptus woods and then pine. Once past a more open section to your right, you will pass through more pine and eucalyptus before reaching a wide cross track. Turn right.

4. Stick to the main track, bearing right at a fork and passing a villa concealed in trees to your right. Shortly after the woods open out,

you will reach a rough road. Keep ahead on to this, passing the Atlantic Riders Lodge) and continuing towards the small village of Monte Novo. The road twists left and then right, passing a number of farm buildings and enclosures. Just past the last enclosure on your right, turn left on to a track signed to Carrapateira.

5. The landscape is now more open, offering views towards the coast. Pass the Nomad Surf Resort and follow the track as it winds downhill to the right. At a fork, take the track turning sharp left. This shortly arrives at another junction, where you again bear left, continuing downhill past an abandoned farm (for sale in October 2015). The track swings to the right by a house and reaches another fork, where you turn left again and descend to wind through a sheltered valley. After a brief climb, the track drops steeply into a dip before climbing back out and passing to the right of a house. Once over the crest of the hill, descend gently into an agricultural landscape dotted with villas and vineyards. Pass the track to Monte dos Cairos on your right and shortly arrive at a main road.

6. Cross the road to a minor road opposite signed to Carrapateira. Follow the road past a number of attractive houses and eventually a scrap yard. About 100 metres past the yard, where the road turns sharply right towards entrance gates, keep ahead on to a dirt vehicle track. This climbs gently along the edge of a stone pine forest before emerging in a more open grassy area and reaching a wide cross track.

7. Keep ahead, joining a gentle descent along a sandy track. Continue down through eucalyptus woods to reach the Bordeira river (usually no more than a small trickle) at the bottom of the valley. Bear right on to a track and follow it down through a lovely open valley and past an isolated farm. Stick to the main track, which bears right at the farm, and shortly cross to the left bank of the stream. Continue down the valley, keeping left at a fork so as to

stay parallel with the main road, which has now appeared across the river to your right.

8. The track leads into the centre of Bordeira village, where it becomes cobbled. At a T-junction opposite a cafe, turn right, then take the next left, passing a sign for Carrapateira opposite the church. Join the next cobbled street on the left, which immediately forks. Take the left-hand road and shortly reach a T-junction with a steep cobbled street ('Travessa do Rampa'). Turn right and then bear left, across the slope. At a junction with a surfaced road (a water tap to the right), keep straight ahead on to the street opposite. When you reach the edge of the village, keep straight up the hill along a concrete track. After passing one final house, the track turns to gravel and begins a long, steep climb away from the village.

9. On reaching a junction of tracks, turn left and climb more gently through stone pine woodland. Bear right at a fork and join a level track to the right of a small lake. Once past the lake, the track bears right and reaches a cross track. Keep straight ahead and descend steeply into a dip. After a short, steep climb, keep straight ahead at the top and descend into a valley through more stone pine forest. Continue down the valley, passing now through an area of more mixed woodland.

10. At a clear fork, descend to the left across the valley. Climb steeply out of the valley to the left and reach a track junction. Turn right, initially on a level track, but soon climbing again. The track crests the brow of the hill and descends into a dip, Carrapateira and the sea now visible to your left. After another small rise, the track continues between fences, the sea and Bordeira beach directly ahead below. Descend towards the coast, passing through the yard of Monte de Cunca – a complex of old farm buildings converted into attractive, environmentally friendly apartments.

11. Reach a T-junction with the main road and turn left towards Carrapateira. As you approach the village, you will pass the Restaurante do Cabrita and a track on the left leading up to the Casa Fajara hotel. Follow the road up into the centre of the village.

Highlight

Carrapateira

Carrapateira is one of the western Algarve's most popular resorts, mainly due to its beaches. To the north of the village is the wide, sandy bay formed by Praia da Bordeira, widely regarded as one of Portugal's best beaches. Further south is another beautiful sandy beach, Praia do Amado, more open to the Atlantic winds and extremely popular with surfers. A waymarked walking route, the Pontal da Carrapateira Circuit (part of the Fishermen's Trail), follows the rugged limestone cliffs between the two bays, providing walkers with an opportunity to explore the local coastal scenery more thoroughly.

For photographs visit www.pinterest.co.uk/thewalkerswife

Day 15: Carrapateira to Vila do Bispo

The climb out of Carrapateira provides good views over Bordeira beach and the rounded, wooded hills extending down to the coast. Lush river valleys then lead inland to Pedralva and the possibility of refreshments. Beyond the village, the trail continues past a wind farm and through a densely wooded valley before emerging into a more open area of scrub and pine. Sandy tracks lead south towards Vila do Bispo and a final descent into the town.

Start: Carrapateira
Finish: Vila do Bispo
Distance: 22km
Total ascent: 299m
Total descent: 206m
Time: 6hrs
Terrain: A relatively flat section along mainly good-quality tracks. Part of the trail along the Carrapateira and Sinceira valleys is prone to flooding following prolonged winter rainfall but can be avoided using an alternative route (this involves another 100m or so of climbing).
Refreshments: About halfway through the section, in the village of Pedralva, is a lovely cafe, bar and restaurant, the Sítio da Pedralva, open every day. Vila do Bispo contains a wide selection of bars, shops and restaurants, including a Lidl supermarket.
Accommodation: The Casa Mestre, the Hotel Mira Sagres and the Pure Flor de Esteva (bed and breakfast) are all located close to the centre of Vila do Bispo, while a five-minute walk from the town is

the Quinta da Pedra. Accommodation is also available about halfway through the section at the Sítio da Pedralva.

Walk instructions

1. Entering Carrapateira from the north, turn left in the village square following a Rota Vicentina sign for Vila do Bispo. Pass the municipal market and bear left up a steep cobbled street. Maintain direction until the road levels off, then turn right into Travessa da Boavista, a little concrete passage between houses. Bear left in front of a house numbered '5', and shortly emerge on a cobbled road opposite a house numbered '1'. Turn left, past the end of the cobbles and on to a tarmac road.

2. Bear right and climb past the Museu do Mar e da Terra da Carrapateira (the Land and Sea Museum). Where the road ends, continue on to a gravel track. This bears right, away from the village, across a slope above the Carrapateira river valley. Keep ahead and join the crest of a ridge. The track continues past masts and a concrete trig point at the top of the hill before winding gently downhill into eucalyptus woods. At a fork, take the track turning sharp left and continue downhill into the Carrapateira valley. Descend until you reach a junction to the right of a house marked private ('Morgado de Aranha').

3. Turn right on to a single-file path. The path passes through thick undergrowth then emerges on the corner of a gravel track. Keep ahead and continue up the valley to a clear fork where the trees open out. Continue ahead along the main lower track to the left, shortly passing to the left of a large villa ('Herdade do Beicudo'). Stick with the main track until you reach a junction with a wider track/road near houses. Turn left here, following a sign for Vilarinha (or right, if staying at Monte do Sapeiro).

4. After about 250 metres, you will reach a junction where the road turns right, in the direction of a sign for an alternative wet weather

route (see below for details). The main route follows the track to the left, however, shortly reaching a fork. Unless staying at Monte da Vilarinha, take the track to the right, signed to Bretanha.

5. Before long, the track draws close to the Carrapateira river, crossing via a ford. It then continues up the narrowing valley, crossing the river twice more. At a fork by a fourth ford, take the right-hand track across the river and join another pleasant valley formed by the Ribeira da Sinceira (generally dry during summer months). The track crosses the riverbed a further two times then meets an access track leading to chalets on the right. Bear left and shortly rejoin the alternative wet weather route, which drops steeply back down to the main route from a dirt track on the right. Continue ahead along the main track to join a road on the edge of Pedralva.

6. The road swings left and then right to reach a junction. Keep straight ahead on to a cobbled street through the village, passing a wooden shelter and benches and then a snack bar and restaurant (the Sítio da Pedralva) on the left. Pass an information board for the Rota Vicentina and continue ahead on to a gravel track leading out of the village. Immediately after a right-hand bend, fork left (i.e. not the drive between palm trees to your right).

7. Continuing down the valley, look out for a waymarked track forking uphill to the right. Follow this up past a farmhouse, keeping straight ahead at a fork and passing to the right of a lake. Climb through eucalyptus woods to reach an area of open scrub to your left. Take a level track forking left across the scrub and reach a triangle of grass below wind turbines. Bear right here and keep ahead at a cross track to reach a junction with the main road between Carrapateira and Vila do Bispo.

8. Keep straight over the road to a track opposite signed to Vila do Bispo. Descend ahead towards an old farm building, then bear right towards a series of waymarks painted on to pine trees (there

is no clear path initially). Join a track to the right of the stone building and descend through trees into a wooded valley. The track is narrow and hemmed in by trees, particularly near the bottom of the valley. Eventually, you will climb out of a dip to reach a junction with a wider track. Turn left here and climb steeply.

9. Shortly after the track levels off you will reach a junction. Turn left and follow a track through open woodland, wind turbines visible on the higher ground ahead. At a clear fork, take the track to the right; this becomes sandy and continues through a mix of scattered pine and eucalyptus trees. At a T-junction with a wide gravel track, turn left and then immediately right to continue on a smaller sandy track. Almost immediately, ignore a track forking right towards derelict buildings; instead, keep ahead along the main track for around 1.6km until you reach a wide cross track near a concrete trig pillar. Keep straight ahead then ahead again at a second cross track, now gradually drawing closer to the main road on your left.

10. At a junction with a wider gravel track (gates and a fence ahead), bear left towards the main road and join a grassy track running parallel to the tarmac. When you reach a cross track, bear left then immediately right to continue on a single-file path marked by posts. This continues on to a grassy verge between a fence and the road. As you pass a house to the right, keep ahead onto a clear track, continuing parallel to the road. After a slight rise, the track starts a gentle descent towards Vila do Bispo, now clearly visible below. Bear left at a fork and join a residential road on the edge of town.

11. Continue ahead, passing to the left of a football ground. Keep ahead at crossroads then ahead again, a short distance ahead, on to a cobbled street. At a T-junction with Rua Capitão Viegas Aviado, take the road bearing slightly left. Almost immediately, the way

ahead is blocked by housing. Take the narrow passage to the left and then turn immediately right, shortly reaching a T-junction opposite a house numbered '7'. Turn left and climb to the top of the hill, where there's a large yellow house directly ahead and a lookout tower peeping above it. Take the cobbled street on the right leading down into the main square. The section ends at the info board in front of the Casa Mestre.

Alternative wet weather route

The track between Vilarinha and Pedralva crosses the Carrapateira and Sinceira rivers a total of six times and after heavy winter rains can get pretty waterlogged. For an alternative route avoiding the fords, follow the signs directing you into the village of Vilarinha. Continue on to a track at the end of the village, then about 200 metres after the last house, turn left on to a path up the hill. At the top, turn right for a short distance then join another dirt track descending steeply to the left. Rejoin the main route in the Sinceira valley and turn right.

Highlight

Pedralva

In 2006, the village of Pedralva, at one time home to over 100 people, had been largely abandoned. Only nine of the original inhabitants still lived in the village and the vast majority of the buildings were in an advanced state of disrepair. Seeing the potential for an innovative tourism project, businessman Antonio Ferreira began to buy up houses in the village and restore them using traditional building techniques. As the project grew, more people came on board and the local council agreed to invest €1m in roads and lighting. As a result, Pedralva has been given a new lease of life and is once again a thriving community.

For photographs visit www.pinterest.co.uk/thewalkerswife

Day 16: Vila do Bispo to Cabo de São Vicente

There are two waymarked routes to Cabo de São Vicente from Vila do Bispo: the Via Algarviana (GR13) and the Rota Vicentina (GR11). The GR11 heads west, making a beeline for the coast at Torre de Aspa before heading south to the finish.

On reaching Ponta Ruiva, there is another choice of routes: the GR11 continues on tracks and lanes across the flat coastal plain while the Fishermen's Trail (the route described) follows a more demanding clifftop route past the Telheiro beach. Both routes rejoin just north of Cabo de São Vicente (together with the Via Algarviana) for a dramatic coastal conclusion to the walk.

Start: Vila do Bispo
Finish: Cabo de São Vicente
Distance: 14km
Total ascent: 126m
Total descent: 133m
Time: 4hrs
Terrain: Fairly level tracks and lanes across an open coastal plain until the start of the Fishermen's Trail at Ponta Ruiva. The second half of the section is more demanding and includes a short ladder descent across a ravine and a tough, undefined route through an area of jumbled rock near Cabo de São Vicente.
Refreshments: A range of snacks and drinks can be bought from stalls outside the fortress at Cabo de São Vicente – though be prepared to pay a premium. There's also a cafe bar inside the fortress.

Accommodation: The nearest accommodation to the end of the trail can be found in Sagres, a short bus journey or 6km walk along the Ecovia do Litoral (see 'Accessing the Via Algarviana' in the Introduction). There's plenty of choice here, but you can also continue on the bus back to Vila do Bispo or on to Lagos – a beautiful city with numerous places to stay.

Walking instructions

1. From the main square in Vila do Bispo, follow the sign for Cabo de S. Vicente towards the top corner of the square to the left of Casa Mestre. Join a road from here heading downhill between the restaurants Solar do Perceve and O Palheiro. Keep straight ahead down the hill and ahead again on to a smaller road where the wider road turns left. On reaching a T-junction with restaurants either side, turn right and follow the road up to a roundabout decorated with statues. Bear left, past the municipal market, and reach a fork in the road either side of the Eira do Mel Restaurante Bar. Take the road to the left of the bar (effectively straight ahead).

2. About 500 metres after the Eira do Mel, look out for a smaller road on the left directly in front of a house called Vivenda do Marinheiro. Join this and immediately follow it round a right-hand bend. Climb gently up to another right-hand bend, after which the road forks. Take the left-hand lane and continue gently uphill. Where the tarmac ends, keep ahead on to a dirt track in the direction of the sea.

3. After passing the gates to Herdade de Lagoa Garcia, the large trig point of Torre de Aspa becomes visible ahead. Just past the trig is a signed junction, from where you may wish to take the detour to the Torre de Aspa viewpoint (1.5km each way) to the right. From here there are excellent views over the Castelejo and Cordoama beaches. The GR11 follows the main track round to the left and starts to head south along the coast. In the distance, the

lighthouse at Cabo de São Vicente now becomes visible for the first time.

4. The track descends gently, passing another signed detour on the right, this time to the Ponta Ruiva viewpoint. After a slight rise, keep right at a fork, ignoring a track bearing left towards a ruin. Eventually reach a signed junction where the main GR11 bears left and the Fishermen's Trail splits off to the right. Join the latter, which immediately passes a track leading down to the Ponta Ruiva beach on the right. Follow the main track round to the left and continue along the top of the cliffs.

5. Where indicated, follow a green waymark arrow on to a smaller track forking right and follow the edge of the cliffs to a small cairn above Praia do Talheiro. Descend along a smaller track towards the bay, then turn left where indicated, away from the sea, and along a narrow, rugged path round the back of the Quebradas ravine (a small wooden ladder is used for the final metre or two of descent down the bank). Climb briefly, then continue on a narrow clifftop path towards the bay. As you approach, look for a waymarked path forking left (or you can continue ahead if you want to descend to the beach).

6. Join the main access track to the beach and turn left, climbing steeply to a car park. From here, bear right towards a stone cairn marking the continuation of the coastal path. After a steep, slightly awkward descent, the path climbs above the bay to a rocky level clifftop where the correct route becomes less clear. Small stone cairns and splashes of paint have been used to mark the route, but these are not always obvious. However, as long as you keep the cliffs to the right and aim for the lighthouse, you can't go too far wrong. After a very rocky section, you should eventually rejoin the route of the Historical Way and Via Algarviana behind a spectacular crescent-shaped bay (look out for the distinctive red-and-white waymarks).

7. Turn right on to a rough stony track above the bay. Initially, this heads directly towards the lighthouse but then bears more to the left and emerges on a main road. Turn right and pass through a large parking area full of food and souvenir stalls. Just in front of the lighthouse you will find a board marking the end of the Rota Vicentina (though, strangely, there is nothing to mark the end of the Via Algarviana). Inside the fort (closed on Mondays) is a supersized chair with the lighthouse behind – a much better spot for an end of walk photograph.

Highlights

Parque Natural do Sudoeste Alentejano e Costa Vicentina

The Southwest Alentejo and Vicentine Coast Natural Park protects a 100km stretch of wild and windswept coastline, from Porto Covo in the Alentejo to Burgau on the southern Algarve coast. The Fishermen's Trail between Ponta Ruiva and Cabo de São Vicente provides a good introduction to the characteristic landscapes of this region: high cliffs protecting a tremendous variety of unspoilt beaches, from tiny rocky coves to glorious sandy bays. While walking, you may be lucky enough to spot a stork nesting along the rocky shoreline or even an osprey hovering above the waves. The exposed coastal cliffs also contain a number of rare plants, some of them unique to the region.

Cabo de São Vicente

Europe's most south-westerly point, Cabo de São Vicente (or Cape St Vincent as it is better known in English) has been regarded as a sacred spot for millennia: the place where the world ended and the sun sank into the ocean. (The cape's spectacular sunsets still draw large crowds of spectators.) In later years, the cape became an important landmark for ships heading for the Mediterranean, and the site of numerous naval battles. A fort was first built on the cape in the 16th century in an attempt to control shipping and protect nearby coastal settlements from raiders (it was rebuilt twice in the 17th and 18th centuries). A primitive lighthouse was also constructed – a crude warning beacon cared for by a group of Franciscan friars living on the cape. This was replaced by the present lighthouse – one of the most powerful in Europe – in 1846.

For photographs visit www.pinterest.co.uk/thewalkerswife

The Via Algarviana: walking 300 km across the Algarve

'The heat was starting to get to us, so when we came to a peaceful spot alongside the Rio Sec we decided it was time to stop for lunch. The shallow stream teemed with tiny darting fish and tadpoles, large azure-coloured dragonflies darted through the air and behind us giant reeds – another invasive species which is now widespread throughout Portugal – swayed in the breeze.

It was such an idyllic spot – and so warm – that I resolved it was time to join Harri and experience my first Algarve dip. Hoisting up the legs of my shorts, I waded cautiously into the cool water and was just thinking I might start doing this kind of thing more often when I spotted something swimming close by. A metre or so from my bare legs was a snake – and it was moving rapidly towards me! Harri, who was already drying off on the dusty river beach, laughed his head off as I frantically splashed my way towards him.'

Follow the author as she hikes the tough, undulating route through the depopulated villages and beautiful mountains of inland Algarve, and gradually succumbs to the charms of a region of rolling hills, dry orchards, cork forests, agricultural terraces and friendly local people.

The Via Algarviana: walking 300 km across the Algarve by Tracy Burton is available from Amazon in ebook and paperback format.

Never too old to backpack: More Algarve hiking

'There was a hurricane heading our way. And because it originated on the other side of the Atlantic, it had a name. It was Monika's mother who alerted her to this depressing news, and Monika shared the news with us.

Hurricane Joaquin first hit the Bahamas and east coast of America; however, now it was heading towards continental Europe, with the worst ravages of the extreme weather forecast for Algarve's west coast – exactly where we were headed tomorrow. Harri warned me to expect rain – and plenty of it – over the next few days. It seemed our 'precautionary' measure of bringing lightweight waterproofs and full-length trousers might not have been precautionary enough.'

Six months after completing the 300km Via Algarviana trail, the author returns to the Algarve to explore more of Portugal's southernmost region on foot.

Away from the popular sandy beaches, the couple tackle several Via Algarviana link routes before heading west to join the wild Atlantic coastline on the Rota Vicentina.

Frequently hiking through spectacular scenery where the only sounds are birdsong and the hum of bees, they encounter vertiginous footpaths, roaming bulls, ravines and rabbits. The real threat, however, is from the fast-approaching Hurricane Joaquin.

Never too old to backpack: More Algarve hiking by Tracy Burton is available from Amazon in ebook and paperback format.

O Fôn i Fynwy: Walking Wales from end to end

'Up to now, perhaps the closest Wales has come to having a genuine end to end walking trail is a popular but unofficial route created by the late Tony Drake. The Cambrian Way is a high-level walk between Cardiff and Conwy which takes in almost all of the principal mountain regions in Wales. Although only 274 miles (441 km) in length, Drake's trail involves almost 19,000 metres of ascent, so is not for the fainthearted. Given fine weather, however, the route is one that almost all mountain walkers will relish.

But here comes the caveat: it rains a lot in Wales, particularly in the mountains. On a long-distance hike of some three to four weeks, there will almost certainly be days of rain and low cloud. In such weather, walking across exposed mountain ridges and high summits is unpleasant at best and at worst plain dangerous.'

The traditional Welsh expression 'O Fôn i Fynwy' literally means from Anglesey (Ynys Môn) to Monmouthshire (Sir Fynwy) but is also used figuratively to mean the whole of Wales, in the same way that 'From Malin to Mizen' is used in Ireland.

By devising a long-distance route which links the two traditional 'ends' of Wales, Harri Garrod Roberts hopes to capture the imagination of long-distance hikers who wish to walk through the most stunning landscapes the country has to offer.

O Fôn i Fynwy: Walking Wales from end to end by Harri Garrod Roberts is available from Amazon's Kindle Store.

Never Too Old To Backpack: a 364-mile walk through Wales

'Predictably, the hills were alive with Duke of Edinburgh participants. I reprimanded Harri when he groaned alongside me. These were our future customers, young people who venture into the wilderness for the first time while still in their teens and resolve to spend the rest of their lives in hiking boots. Only the majority of this lot looked pretty miserable under the weight of their huge rucksacks; worse, despite having barely left their valley campsite, they were huddling together in that all too familiar way. They couldn't be lost already, Harri sighed.'

Never too old to backpack: a 364-mile walk through Wales is a personal account of the author's experience of walking the undulating and frequently mountainous O Fôn i Fynwy route from Holyhead to Chepstow devised by Harri Garrod Roberts.

From a sleepless night on a Bronze Age settlement to meltdown in Llandovery, a hunt for a long-lost friend in Beddgelert to karaoke in Brecon, Tracy Burton shares the very best (and worst) that Wales – and long-distance hiking – has to offer.

Never too old to backpack: a 364-mile walk through Wales is available from Amazon in ebook and paperback format.

Other books by Harri Garrod Roberts

Print books

Day Walks in the Brecon Beacons (Vertebrate Publishing)

Day Walks in Pembrokeshire National Park (Vertebrate Publishing)

Carmarthen Bay & Gower: Circular Walks along the Wales Coast Path (Northern Eye Books)

Carmarthenshire & Gower: Wales Coast Path Official Guide (Tenby to Swansea) (Northern Eye Books)

Digital books

Dylan's Welsh Walks

Castle Walks in Monmouthshire

Castle Walks in the Marches of Gwent

Castle Walks around Newport and Cardiff

Rhymney Valley Walks

Circular Walks on the Gower Peninsula

England Coast Path: Severn Estuary & Bridgwater Bay

About the author

Harri Garrod Roberts has an academic background in literary studies and Welsh culture, including both an MA and a PhD in Welsh writing in English.

He is a fluent Welsh speaker and works as a freelance writer, translator, editor, book reviewer and proof reader.

He has published several Welsh hiking guides with traditional publishers and has written many more digital guidebooks with his partner, Tracy Burton. This is his first European guidebook.

Harri is passionate about hiking and believes that some of the most stunning natural landscapes and trails remain undiscovered by hikers.

His hiking guides are easy to follow, and are written with both experienced long-distance hikers and those who just want to enjoy a day's hiking in beautiful surroundings in mind.

Get in touch

The instructions in this guidebook were accurate when they were written; however, landscapes are always evolving. If you do encounter problems on any section of the Via Algarviana, please email me at roberts.harri@gmail.com

In fact, if you have feedback of any kind, I'm always very happy to hear from you.

In the meantime, Tracy and I hope you enjoy exploring the spectacular scenery and white-washed villages of the inland Algarve as much as we did.

Printed in Great Britain
by Amazon